THE EXCELLENCE OF CHRIST—
AN ENCOUNTER WITH THE SAVIOR

CAS MONACO

THE EXCELLENCE OF CHRIST

AN ENCOUNTER WITH THE SAVIOR

A devotional Bible study
on the book of Hebrews

Entrusting God's Treasure
To The Faithful

Entrusting God's Treasure To The Faithful
101 Finsbury Lane
Durham, NC 27703
(919) 667-8268
Cas.Monaco@uscm.org
www.entrusting.org

First printing, January 2009

Cover design by Marci Hafer,
dailydesign@hotmail.com

Dedication

With open hands I lay this labor of love at the feet of my Savior and gratefully acknowledge His grace and wonderful counsel that enabled me to learn and persevere to the end. In addition to completing the study, I humbly worship Him for the rich display of His excellent and beautiful character woven throughout Hebrews. May we all encounter Jesus in fresh ways through the study of His Word.

CONTENTS

ACKNOWLEDGMENTS

One friend said, "It doesn't take a village to create a Bible study, but it does take a team." I agree. My teammate and love of my life, Bob, is my number-one champion. He urges, motivates, and encourages me to "excel still more" even if it affects him, which it often does. Then, without the help of Kristi, Sarita, Becky, Amy, Ilje, Marian, Delane, Laura, Janean, and Shana, I'd still be halfway finished with this study. I need, and appreciate, Cara, Shana, and Terri's tireless commitment to grammatical correctness. Marci persevered with me until we found the perfect cover to reflect the heart of the study and the message of Hebrews. Tyler brings all of the pages of words to life by formatting everything into a readable format. Everyone represented gave of their time in the midst of serving the Lord, raising their families, going to their "real" jobs, and living life. Without this team of men and women, this manuscript would be half-finished in my computer.

THE EXCELLENCE OF CHRIST

As I grow older in the Lord, I find myself longing for a clearer view of Jesus. I read my Bible and seem to gravitate toward the Gospels so that I can hear His wise words and watch Him interact with the sick and blind and destitute, the proud and skeptical, and the crazed demons (the only ones who, for a time, really knew who He was). He called His followers to lose their lives for His sake, to take up their cross daily and follow, and to die and bear fruit. He led the way by shedding His blood and by giving His life to pay for the sins of the world—as a demonstration of His great love. Recently, I had a conversation with a college freshman, who upon hearing about Jesus and His love said, "I've never heard of such a love before." There is no doubt—the love of Jesus is beyond compare.

What compels me, as I walk with Him, is this love. This incredible love was part of God's plan right from the very beginning of time and is woven throughout all the pages of Scripture. God, creatively and purposefully, began paving the way for the coming of Christ in the earliest chapters of Genesis. Many people and events in the Old Testament foreshadow the person and work of Jesus Christ—who is at the center of it all right from the beginning.

My hope and prayer is that as we study this book together, Jesus Christ will become infinitely more attractive as we gaze into His face and marvel at His sovereign plan.

The book of Hebrews was written somewhere between A.D. 70 and A.D. 90 and was addressed to Jewish believers in Rome. It's assumed the recipients were primarily (though not exclusively as we will see) Jewish believers because so much of the information contained in the letter pertains to the Jewish law, priesthood, and sacrificial system. It's important to note that these Christians lived under great fear of persecution during this span of time. Nero, the Roman emperor of the day, was a self-centered and cruel leader. For example, in the spring of A.D. 64 a raging fire swept through Rome. Nero, because he wanted to rebuild Rome his own way, was accused of setting fire to the city himself. In order to dispel these rumors, he accused followers of Christ of starting the fire and mercilessly persecuted many..."'Mockery of every sort was added to their deaths. Covered with the skins of beasts, they were torn by dogs and perished, or were nailed to crosses, or were doomed to the flames and burnt, to serve as a nightly illumination, when daylight had expired.'" [1] I can imagine that believers who lived in Rome often feared for their lives and were quite possibly tempted to question or even hide their Christian faith.

Hebrews was written by an unnamed and unknown author whom many believe to be the apostle Paul. Although Paul was called by God to take the Gospel to the Gentiles, he was passionate about his kinsmen—the Jews—hearing the Gospel and believing in Christ as Messiah. Some researchers believe the author was Barnabas, Alexander, or Priscilla, all faithful followers of Jesus during the time in which the letter was written. For some reason, the Holy Spirit doesn't reveal the human "pen" of this Epistle. But whoever did write it cared deeply about those to whom the letter was written. In addition, this person had extraordinary insight into the person and work of Jesus Christ from which believers throughout the ages have benefitted greatly.

The writer of Hebrews begins the book by exalting Christ Jesus as God's final word and continues by proclaiming His superiority over the most prominent Old Testament leaders, the Law, the priesthood, and the sacrificial and ceremonial systems of the Jewish faith. Believers are encouraged to rest in the finished work of Jesus at the cross and are exhorted to stand firm, press on, and hold fast to Him in the face of persecution, doubt, and the daily temptation to sin—all based upon the beauty of the New Covenant in Jesus Christ. In addition, throughout the letter the writer warns unbelievers and points them to the Savior and the seriousness of salvation.

Over the years, as I take time to read and meditate on Hebrews, I step away exclaiming with a whisper, "Wow, what a Savior!"

My hope and prayer is that as we study this book together, Jesus Christ will become infinitely more attractive as we gaze into His face and marvel at His sovereign plan. Hebrews provides a great overview of the Old Testament, the law, the priesthood, and sacrificial system as it points to Jesus. As an old Bible teacher once told me, "If you can get a handle on Hebrews, you can get a handle on the whole Bible." As I prepared this study guide, I realized I will never plumb the depths of this challenging and complex book of Scripture. One thing is certain, the vast treasure and rich truth available in Hebrews will keep you and I digging for a long time.

---

1 Wikipedia, *Nero* (Online at http://en.wikipedia.org/wiki/Nero).

Encountering the Savior
An Overview

The study of Hebrews will challenge you on a variety of levels; therefore, I encourage you to pray that the Holy Spirit will guide and teach you all along the way.

Each lesson is broken down into five days that you can work on throughout the week. Days One, Two, and Four will walk you through the passage we're studying that week. I ask questions that will help you look at the passage and discern for yourself what is being said. From time to time, I insert comments and more information to help you as you study. Throughout the study I'll give suggestions and ideas regarding prayer, worship, evangelism, and your walk with the Lord. I also include "For Further Study" sections to aid you in a more in-depth study of a particular topic.

Day Three is called "Digging Deeper," which generally focuses on a truth contained in the week's passage. Day Five is set aside either to catch up on or reflect upon what you've learned that week. Periodically I'll insert a suggestion "For Further Study" that you can choose to do along with your study now or save it for another time.

Each day I remind you to read through Hebrews. Over the years I've found that reading and rereading a book of Scripture has helped me more than any other form of Bible study. It has always been a great way to imprint the passage and eventually the whole book into my mind and heart, and ultimately it helps me understand the meaning of the book. Quite honestly, Hebrews is not easy to understand right away. It will take time to grasp the concepts. So reading and rereading it will help you comprehend its rich truths. I remind you at the beginning of each day to read as much as you're able. You'll be glad you did—I promise.

Throughout this study, I encourage you to write down verses, thoughts, and prayers. I often do this myself in a journal because I like processing with the Lord as I write. I encourage you to keep a journal of your discoveries and thoughts over the next several weeks. Bookstores and office stores sell leather- and fabric-bound journals, and Target or Wal-Mart carry spiral-bound notebooks. Purchase whatever style best suits you. I can't tell you the number of times I've actually gone back and read from my journals when I wanted to remember what the Lord was teaching me during a particular season of my life.

Father, thank You for Your Word that is perfect and restores our souls, makes us wise, and brings joy to our hearts amid the trials and tribulations of our earthly lives. We're so aware we live in a world that is corroded, dark, and temporal. Thank You for giving us Your Word that is pure and clean and everlasting—like You. Create in us a longing for the sweet richness of Your instruction and keep our hearts soft and pliable in order to receive Your warnings. Thank You, Holy Spirit, for being our Teacher and our Guide. What a marvel that You live in our hearts as our Helper. Give us Your wisdom and understanding as we embark on this journey through Hebrews. Help us to fall more in love with Jesus Christ—the author and perfecter of our faith. In His name and for His glory.

DAY ONE

☐ Read Hebrews

The best way to familiarize yourself with a book of Scripture is to read it all the way through in one sitting. It's important, and helpful, to see the context within the big picture of the book. Although Hebrews, with 13 chapters, is a hefty book, I encourage you to read it in one sitting to start. Don't be discouraged if it doesn't make a lot of sense, or you're distracted, or you fall asleep. It takes time to understand and focus. After you've read it through once, take it a few chapters at a time each time you sit down to study. Either way, try to read it through consistently. I am confident by the time you're halfway through this study, the book will begin to make a lot more sense. So, that's where we'll begin. Ask the Lord to give you clarity and focus as you read.

1. As you read through Hebrews, record some of the words, passages, verses, and/or concepts that jumped out to you.

2. You might have questions that surface as a result of reading through the book. Record those questions in your notebook. It's my hope that by the time you complete the study most of your questions will be answered, and if they're not you'll have a good foundation from which to do further study on your own.
   Here are some of the questions I've had:
   • Who in the world is Melchizedek?
   • Are angels real?
   • Can I lose my salvation?
   • What is a tabernacle?

3.　Whether this is your first time studying Hebrews or you've enjoyed its truths for a long time, it's always intriguing and exciting to begin a new study of God's Word. What are you looking forward to as you begin this pursuit, and what do you hope to gain? If this is your first Bible study, maybe you're simply hoping to understand more about Jesus or your salvation. If you're in a group perhaps you're looking forward to getting to know other believers better, or maybe you're looking for something to help you consistently read or pray. Whatever it is, write it down.

Reflect & Respond

Hebrews 13:15 says, "Through Him then, let us continually offer up a sacrifice of praise to God, this is, the fruit of lips that give thanks to His name."

ⓒ Before you close your Bible and move on to the next thing in your day or evening, take a minute and thank the Lord for what you read today—whether it made complete sense or not. Thank Him for the freedom to read His Word and study it either alone or with others. Thank Him for His Son—the heir of all things and Creator. Then, tell Him what you're hoping to gain and what you're looking forward to as you dig into Hebrews.

ⓒ As you face the day or reflect on what has already happened, thank the Lord for the events, conversations, frustrations, and opportunities that He brought your way. Thankfulness is an expression of faith in the One who is intimately acquainted with all our ways and numbers our steps along the ups and downs of life.

A word about the Word

As a young believer, I was influenced by a little book Robert Shirock wrote entitled, *Studying God's Word and Loving It.* He encouraged his readers to choose a reliable translation and purchase a good, sturdy Bible that is enjoyable to pick up and read and that will be around for a long time.

My Bible-reading friends encouraged me to choose a readable format I could stay with for my lifetime. They explained to me that I would become more and more familiar with my Bible and would easily be able to recall certain verses or passages because I could "picture" the page in my mind. They were right! I've used the same Bible for a long time and often, when I can't remember a chapter or verse, I usually can remember the general location of the verse.

Let me encourage you to find a Bible you're comfortable with and one you will look forward to reading. Collect a few extras that are the same format, just in case your first one wears out! I am sure you will reap the same rewards I have.

Also, in this study I most often use the *New American Standard Bible*, but there are other translations like the New International or English Standard Bible that are good for study. Often, I'll use other translations because they're easier to understand. I suggest you start with at least one good study Bible and add paraphrased versions to your library over time. You can never have enough Bibles!

DAY TWO

☐ Read Hebrews 1-4

Due to the title and content of Hebrews, it's clear most of the recipients of this epistle (letter) were Jewish Christians, and they were struggling with giving up the Jewish Law and sacrificial system that had been in place for centuries. The writer goes to great lengths to point out the reasons Jesus Christ and the New Covenant are superior to (better or more excellent than) the Old Covenant, and at the same time he explains in detail why the Law was given to Moses in the Old Testament, the priesthood begun in Exodus, and the sacrificial system described at length in Leviticus (explained more as we go) were a copy or a shadow of what was ultimately fulfilled in Jesus Christ. So, let's do an overview of what's to come.

1. Notice that a major theme in Hebrews is the fact that Jesus Christ is superior to (better or more excellent than) anything having to do with the Old Covenant or the Law.

    a. Look at the following verses and record what you learn about Jesus.
       Hebrews 1:2-3

       Hebrews 2:14-18

       Hebrews 3:1, 2 and 6

    b. Jesus Christ is superior to who or what?
       Hebrews 1:4

       Hebrews 3:3

2. Hebrews 4:1-8 talks about Jesus bringing about a superior rest. We'll look at this more closely later, but according to Hebrews 4:9-10, what do you learn about the rest that is ours in Christ?

3. In a sermon on Hebrews, Tim Keller (pastor of Redeemer Presbyterian Church in New York City) takes note that on the one hand, Hebrews is bursting with encouragement, and on the other hand, it is full of strong warnings. Read the following and record either the encouragement or the warning:

    Hebrews 2:1

    Hebrews 3:12-13

    Hebrews 4:11

    Hebrews 4:16

Reflect & Respond

Whether there's warning or encouragement, what strikes me as I read and study this book is the fact that Jesus is at the heart of Hebrews. He is grand and majestic, holy and righteous, the Creator and King; and at the same time, He is full of mercy and grace. He invites us to rest our weary souls at the foot of His lovely throne.

@ What keeps you from drawing near to His throne of grace?

© After gazing into His face through the book of Hebrews today, what about Him encourages you to draw near despite your hesitation?

Sometimes reading Scripture aloud really helps me "hear" the Lord through His Word more clearly above the din of my mind's haphazard thoughts. So, throughout the study I'll encourage you to read a passage aloud to potentially help you worship or guide you as you pray. You might feel silly or self-conscious, but try it a few times and see if it doesn't help you concentrate more.

© Read Hebrews 1:1-4 and 4:14-16 aloud. Praise His greatness and majesty along with His mercy and grace. Thank Him that He is always there to help in time of need.

DAY THREE

☐ Read Hebrews 5-10

We'll continue our overview of Hebrews by looking at chapters 5-10. The questions on today's lesson are the same as yesterday's. Keep in mind that this is just a broad overview of Hebrews, and we'll get more in-depth as the study progresses. If questions arise, which they probably will, jot them down in the back of your study.

Remember to pray before you begin. Ask the Holy Spirit to guide and teach you as you walk through the next few chapters.

1. Read Hebrews 5-10.

2. A major theme in Hebrews is the fact that Jesus Christ is superior to (better or more excellent than) anything having to do with the Old Covenant or the Law. The following questions will help you discover why.

   a. Look at the following verses and record one or two things you learn about the person of Jesus:
      Hebrews 5:7-10

      Hebrews 6:19-20

      Hebrews 7:24-28

   b. Who or what is Jesus Christ superior to?
      Hebrews 4:15-5:9; 7:23-28

      Hebrews 8:4-6

Hebrews 9:11-15 (9:23-28)

Hebrews 10:1-4; 10:11-14

3. Step back from your work and take a good long look at Jesus—your Savior. What stands out to you personally as you look at Him in these passages and why (refer back to Day Two, as well)?

4. Hebrews bursts with encouragement and/or strong warnings. Read the following and record either the encouragement or the warning:

    Hebrews 6:1

    Hebrews 6:9-12

    Hebrews 10:19-25

    Hebrews 10:32-39

Reflect & Respond

It seems, from the encouragement and warning found in these first ten chapters, the believers during this period of time experienced persecution, doubt, distraction, temptation, conflict, and hopelessness.

Sound familiar? On top of that, the very foundation of their religious beliefs and practices had been turned upside down—all for something much better. However, the challenges were enormous. This letter, inspired by the Holy Spirit of God, shows us how He deeply cares for His children by providing exhortation and encouragement.

@ How have you experienced His encouragement this week? Express your thanks by writing a prayer in your journal.

DAY FOUR

☐ Read Hebrews 11-13

"Therefore, do not throw away your confidence, which has a great reward. For you have need of endurance, so that when you have done the will of God, you may receive what was promised. **For yet in a very little while, He who is coming will come, and will not delay. But My righteous one shall live by faith; and if he shrinks back, My soul has no pleasure in him.** But we are not of those who shrink back to destruction, but of those who have faith to the preserving of the soul" (Hebrews 10:35-39, emphasis added).

This great exhortation leads us right into what is known as the "Great Hall of Faith." The writer reflects on the history of men and women "of old" who triumphed by faith in God in the face of all kinds of challenges and kept a hopeful eye toward "a better country, that is a heavenly one" (Hebrews 11:16).

1. Read and write out the following verses that define faith:

    Hebrews 11:1

    Hebrews 11:6

2. Scan chapter 11 and record the various people the writer uses as examples of faith.

3. Chapters 12 and 13 wrap up the letter with practical instruction—instruction that describes a life of faith—but begins with Jesus.

    a. Read and write out Hebrews 12:1-3.

b. Why do you think the writer exhorts us to "fix our eyes on Jesus" according to Hebrews 12:2?

4. With our eyes fixed on Jesus, look at the following passages and record some of the topics the writer touches on:

Hebrews 12:7

Hebrews 12:14-15

Hebrews 13:1-5

Hebrews 13:7, 17

Hebrews 13:9-12

Reflect & Respond

ⓐ Hebrews 13:20-21 is a good "purpose statement" for the great instruction we will receive from Hebrews. Make it your prayer as you conclude your study (here's an example):

I praise you O God of peace. Thank you for raising the Great Shepherd of the sheep—Jesus our Lord. Thank You for my salvation and the relationship I so enjoy because of Your great sacrifice. I praise You for the blood of the covenant (and look forward to learning more). Equip me in every good thing dear Jesus. Work in me, through the work of the Spirit, that which is pleasing in Your sight—for Your glory forever and ever.

DAY FIVE

Reflection

This overview of Hebrews whets my appetite for more. I hope the same is true for you. We've covered a lot of ground this week—13 chapters of the Bible! Throughout our study, Day Five is reserved for reflection and catch up. I will generally guide you through a review of the week's lesson and sometimes lead you through a time of worship.

Here are some suggestions as you wrap up this lesson:

1. If you haven't had a chance to finish reading Hebrews, then today is a good day to catch up. Remember, even if it doesn't make complete sense, or you fall asleep, or find your brain a million miles away, keep going. Soon it will begin to fall into place—I promise.

2. If you have already finished reading Hebrews….you might reflect over the week's lesson. Maybe certain chapters or verses stuck out to you. Go back and read them again. The Holy Spirit might be shining His light in that very spot of Hebrews just for you. If you have time and the inkling, explore the passage or other parts of the Bible that He's showing you.

3. Or you could read Hebrews 1:1-3 aloud (again) and meditate on Jesus. Think about what the verses say about Him and how He impacts the universe, the world, your life. Praise Him for His awesome greatness.

4. If you have more questions, remember to write those down in the back of your study.

For Further Study

Throughout Hebrews we'll discover many of God's attributes. An attribute is a characteristic that is perfectly true of God. One of God's characteristics found in Hebrews 1:3 is that He is omnipotent—omni: all; potent: powerful.

The following verses tell us about His omnipotence:

- I Chronicles 29:11-13

- Job 42:1-2

- Isaiah 40:25-26

- Matthew 19:26

How does knowing God is omnipotent encourage you in your present circumstances?

Jesus, God's Final Word

Hebrews 1:1-3

More than ever before, because of the Internet, I'm acutely aware of the chaotic events that ravage the inhabitants of the world every day. The violent and never-ending devastation in Iraq, the turbulence in Israel, the crisis in Sudan, and earthquakes and hurricanes relentlessly take thousands of lives in remote parts of this world that grows smaller by the day. The global economy seems to hang by a thread—every day the report is different. When I narrow my field of observation to the lives in my neighborhood or within my acquaintances, friends, or family, or consider my own life, I often see difficulty, challenges beyond measure, and sadness. I feel compelled to add that for those who follow Jesus blessing, joy, richness, and community result from these trials of life. However the reality still holds—life on earth is rarely easy.

The recipients of the Hebrew letter faced harassment and maltreatment beyond my imagination. Weary of life's complexities, they were persuaded to wonder where is God in all of this, is He there, does He care, if He really loves us then why is everything so hard? In chapter 10, the writer reminds them at a point in time they persevered in the face of persecution and exhorts them to continue to walk by faith. It's important to remember that most of the recipients of this letter were Jewish believers who were tempted to hearken back to Abraham and Moses, Aaron and the Levitical Priesthood, and the Law as being somehow better than Jesus Christ.

The writer, fully aware of their heart and mindset, implores the readers to pay attention, take care, be encouraged, rest, beware, be diligent and confident, press on, draw near, hold fast, and ultimately to be fixed on Jesus. Inspired by God's Spirit, the writer lifts up the name of Jesus as the matchless, supreme, majestic Savior, who is better than anything else that might capture their attention. He is sovereign over the universe, aware and in charge of every event around the globe, and intimately acquainted with all of their ways. As I fast-forward to the 21st century, it encourages me to know that Jesus Christ is sovereign over the wars and rumors of wars, the hurricanes, tornados and earthquakes, and a poor economy. Jesus is intimately acquainted with all of my ways and yours. He is worthy of our worship and trust.

In this lesson we're going to take a good, long look at Jesus Christ. What's so amazing about Jesus? Who is He and what sets Him apart? Why is He superior or better?

As you begin your time with the Lord in Hebrews, ask His Spirit to free your mind from distractions and to prepare your heart to meet with your Savior.

DAY ONE

☐ Read Hebrews

Hebrews 1:1-4

All day long I've meditated on Hebrews 1:1-4. I sat with the Lord under a bright morning sky and listened to music that lifted my heart to worship the King, my Savior. I felt blessed to actually know the God who created the cloudy wisps painted across the heavens, the hummingbirds that flit through the air, and the smell of the fir trees in the soft summer breeze. Then, a few hours later—the Lord still on my heart and mind—I overheard a very interesting conversation at my hair salon. While getting her hair cut, a woman sitting nearby told her stylist with great conviction and exuberance about her worship of animals. Much like I would share how God has changed my life, she described the life-giving blessings she's received as a result of her faith in creation.

On the one hand I was dumbstruck and amazed by her testimony and her lifelong commitment to her beliefs. On the other hand, I couldn't help but think of Romans 1:25, "For they exchanged the truth of God for a lie, and worshiped and served the creature rather than the Creator."

In his book *Seeing and Savoring Jesus Christ,* John Piper writes, "We were made to know and treasure the glory of God above all things; and when we trade that treasure for images, everything is disordered… The healing of the soul begins by restoring the glory of God to its flaming, all-attracting place at the center."[1] I left the salon sobered by the seriousness of knowing the Creator and resolved to know Him more intimately. Hebrews starts at the center: God and Jesus Christ. I remember memorizing the first three verses of Hebrews long ago, but every time I come back to this short passage, I'm struck by the magnificence of Jesus Christ as well as the plan of God that stretches all the way back to before Creation.

Enjoy your time in the Word as you begin by looking at the glory of God displayed in Jesus the Son.

1. Read Hebrews 1:1-4.

2. According to Hebrews 1:1, God spoke long ago to the fathers through the prophets—Moses being the first through whom God gave the Ten Commandments (the Law) at Mount Sinai recorded in Exodus. The next prophets to come onto the scene were Elijah and Elisha. Then, 17 more prophets whose words were directed toward either the kingdom of Israel or the kingdom of Judah. Their messages include both hope and judgment, ultimately foretelling the coming of Jesus Christ and "telling forth" impending judgment for their disobedience.

   a. According to I Peter 1:10-12 & II Peter 1:20-21, what do you learn about the prophets and the angels?

b. Who were they ultimately serving?

3. Read Hebrews 1:2. Through whom has God spoken to us in these last days?

4. a. Based upon what you've learned, describe the differences between the ways God spoke long ago through the prophets with the ways He has spoken to us through His Son.

b. Why are these differences significant?

Reflect & Respond

Moses was the first of God's prophets. He listened and talked to God on behalf of the children of Israel. As they fled Egypt, they could see a visible manifestation of God in the pillar of cloud by day and a pillar of fire at night. Later, after the tabernacle was erected God's presence would burn in all its brilliant glory in the Holy of Holies, but there was no personal communication without a mediator (which we'll learn more about later in Hebrews). Nobody could look upon God and live.

I was always afraid of God. He felt very stern and very far away, and I felt very unworthy—until I placed my faith in Jesus. I remember the day I asked Christ to be my Savior and the freedom that came with forgiveness. I also remember realizing that He listens to my prayers and wants me to talk to Him about everything because we have a relationship. Wow, what a Savior!

@ What does it mean to you, right now, to know that you have a relationship with God's Son? What difference has it made in your life to have a relationship with Him?

What a privilege it is to live during a time when God no longer speaks to us through prophets, but directly through His Son. Christ beautifully pictures God's desire for a personal relationship and intimate communion with you and me. I love how one commentator put it, "Life with a capital 'L' has come into our midst". [2]

DAY TWO

☐ Read Hebrews

Hebrews 1:2-4

In these last days, God has spoken to us through His living, breathing, flesh-on-bones Son. It's hard to grasp the fact that God became man, isn't it? I love that Hebrews 1:2 says, "He is the exact representation of God's nature." If we want to know what God is like, all we have to do is look at and listen to Jesus. As you dig into these few verses, pray that you'll have eyes to see Jesus Christ with a renewed and fresh understanding.

1. Write down the things that are true of Jesus in Hebrew 1:2-4 (in my translation there are eight).

   a. He is God's Son (Hebrews 1:2)

   b.

   c.

   d.

   e.

   f.

   g.

   h. He sits at the right hand of the Majesty on high. (Hebrews 1:3)

It's so encouraging to remember the Bible has 66 books and was written by 40 different authors (all inspired by God's Spirit) over a period of 3,500 years. We have the privilege of seeing the whole Redemption story fulfilled in Jesus Christ, who has fulfilled the "prophetic word" spoken long ago. In this next section, we're going to take the characteristics of Jesus listed in Hebrews 1:1-3 and look at the Old Testament prophecies and the New Testament fulfillment of those prophecies.

2. Look at the following passages and record what you learn about the Son of God. I've included verses and passages from the Old Testament that point toward the coming of Jesus and verses and passages in the New Testament where God speaks through His Son.

    a. Prophetic Word/Old Testament
       Jesus, God's Son (Hebrews 1:1)

       Psalm 2:7; Isaiah 7:14

    b. God speaking in His Son
       John 1:14

3. Read Romans 1:1-4. What powerful event declared Jesus to be the Son of God?

4. Why does it matter that Jesus is the Son of God and not just another prophet or some kind of a religious leader?

5. What does it mean that Jesus is both heir (rightful inheritor) of all things and Creator (Hebrews 1:2)? See the following for insight:

    a. Prophetic Word/Old Testament
       Isaiah 66:1-2

    b. God speaking through His Son/New Testament
       John 1:1-3

       Revelation 21:3-7

6. Consider something that you're facing personally, like in your family or in your job. What difference does it or can it make to know that the Son of God (your Savior) is the heir of all things and the Creator of the universe?

Reflect & Respond

This truth can seem distant and impersonal until we bring all of who Jesus is into the realm of our daily lives. It makes a difference in the face of misunderstandings, work-related deadlines, grim health reports, or family drama to know Jesus Christ is God. He not only reigns as King and Creator, but He is also God's Son, our Savior. Nothing in the universe is beyond His control or care, and at the same time, He listens to our cries and enters into our distress.

It's incredible that the whole plan of redemption began long before the world ever was. Jesus Christ is eternal and reigns as King of kings and Lord of lords. Tom Wright in his commentary, *Hebrews for Everyone*, explains, "In the message of the gospel the King himself has come to speak to us directly…and when the message was preached things happened—signs, wonders, mighty deeds, presumably healing, but perhaps other things too, sudden conversions, the transformation of families, synagogue communities, villages." [3]

@ What evidence is there in your own life, and in your church, that the gospel message of Jesus is true and powerful?

DAY THREE

DIGGING DEEPER

As I mentioned in the Introduction, Day Three is reserved for Digging Deeper into a truth pertaining to our study. We'll continue our look at Hebrews 1:1-4 in Day Four, but today we're going to walk through Psalm 33 and respond to God in worship. I love the Psalms, because the writers often expressed their feelings of need and desperation while recognizing and finding comfort. in the magnificence of God. I've learned a lot about what it means to walk with the Lord through the "hard stuff of life" by reading and spending time in this great book of the Bible. In addition, it's filled with historical references that help us understand Israel's past—and the book of Hebrews.

The psalmist in Psalm 33 praises God as the Creator of all things and at the same time brings Him into our level of life and reality. I like to read a Psalm aloud to the Lord and often personalize it by inserting myself into the passage. Then I read it as though I were talking directly to the Lord. I've included *The New Living Translation* here.

Psalm 33
¹ Let the godly sing for joy to the LORD;
it is fitting for the pure to praise him.
² Praise the LORD with melodies on the lyre;
make music for him on the ten-stringed harp.
³ Sing a new song of praise to him;
play skillfully on the harp, and sing with joy.
⁴ For the word of the LORD holds true,
and we can trust everything he does.
⁵ He loves whatever is just and good;
the unfailing love of the LORD fills the earth.
⁶ The LORD merely spoke,
and the heavens were created.
He breathed the word,
and all the stars were born.
⁷ He assigned the sea its boundaries
and locked the oceans in vast reservoirs.
⁸ Let the whole world fear the LORD,
and let everyone stand in awe of him.
⁹ For when he spoke, the world began!
It appeared at his command.

¹⁰ The Lord frustrates the plans of the nations
and thwarts all their schemes.
¹¹ But the Lord's plans stand firm forever;
his intentions can never be shaken.
¹² What joy for the nation whose God is the Lord,
whose people he has chosen as his inheritance.
¹³ The Lord looks down from heaven
and sees the whole human race.
¹⁴ From his throne he observes
all who live on the earth.
¹⁵ He made their hearts,
so he understands everything they do.
¹⁶ The best-equipped army cannot save a king,
nor is great strength enough to save a warrior.
¹⁷ Don't count on your warhorse to give you victory—
for all its strength, it cannot save you.
¹⁸ But the Lord watches over those who fear him,
those who rely on his unfailing love.
¹⁹ He rescues them from death
and keeps them alive in times of famine.
²⁰ We put our hope in the Lord.
He is our help and our shield.
²¹ In him our hearts rejoice,
for we trust in his holy name.
²² Let your unfailing love surround us, Lord,
for our hope is in you alone.

1.   a. Look for things that are true of Him in Psalm 33:4-5. For example, His Word holds true. We can trust whatever He does, and His unfailing love fills the earth (How awesome is that?). Circle more things that you discover about Him.

b. Stop to thank and praise Him for who He is.
  • *Thank You that Your Word holds true and that I can trust You with everything You do.*
  • *I praise You for Your unfailing love that fills the earth.*
  • *Take some of the truths that you've circled and praise Him.*

2. a. What do you discover to be true about God's view of the earth, its inhabitants, the generations?

  b. In light of the turbulent times we're living in, how does this discovery make you feel?

3. "But the LORD watches over those who fear him, those who rely on his unfailing love."

  a. What does it mean to both "fear" Him and rely on His love?

  b. How does the psalmist respond in verses 21 and 22?

4.   How does this Psalm encourage you in your own journey with Jesus?

5.   After you've observed and considered the rich truths in this Psalm, read it aloud again. This time praise Him for the way you've seen Him at work in your own life, or pray for those around you who need a fresh glimpse of His unfailing love or some other aspect of who He is.

DAY FOUR

☐ Read Hebrews

Hebrews 1:3-4

"God…in these last days has spoken to us in His Son, whom He appointed heir of all things, through whom also He made the world" (Hebrews 1:1-2). He speaks to us and initiates a relationship with us through Jesus Christ. What an honor. As you continue to refresh your understanding of Him today, pray that the Lord will free you from distraction and keep your heart and mind focused.

Jesus, The Radiance of God's Glory (Hebrews 1:3)

1. What do you learn about the glory of God from these Old and New Testament passages?

    a. Prophetic Word/Old Testament
       Exodus 33:18-23

       Isaiah 6:1-5

    b. God speaking through His Son/New Testament
       John 17:1-5

       II Corinthians 3:18, 4:3-4

Jesus, The Exact Representation of His Nature (Hebrews 1:3)

2. Record what you observe about the nature of God from both the Old and New Testament.

    a. Prophetic Word/Old Testament
       Psalm 23

Isaiah 11:1-5

b. God speaking through His Son/New Testament

"No one has ever seen God; the only God, who is at the Father's side, He has made Him known" (John 1:18 ESV). I love this verse because it reminds me that anytime I want to understand God or see what He's like all I have to do is look into the face of His only Son—Jesus Christ. The Gospel of John paints a beautiful picture of the nature of God as Jesus interacts with all different kinds of people in all different types of settings. The following passages give us a glimpse into the heart of God reflected in Jesus. Record your observations (If you have time, read each chapter for a fuller picture of the context).
John 4:10, 13-14

John 10:14-15

Jesus Upholds All Things by the Word of His Power (Hebrews 1:3)

3. a. According to John 1:1 Jesus is "the Word," and "the Word was God." In I John 1:1 He is called "the Word of Life." Keep these verses in mind and look at Hebrews 4:12.

    b. How does this verse enhance your understanding of the power of Christ's word?

    c. Prophetic Word/Old Testament
    Psalm 33:6-9

    Isaiah 55:10-11

d. God speaking through His Son/New Testament
Colossians 1:16-17

Revelation 19:11-16

Jesus Made Purification of Sins (Hebrews 1:3)

4. Look at the following passages and record what you learn about our need for purification and how Jesus Christ provides it.

a. Prophetic Word/Old Testament
Isaiah 53

b. God speaking through His Son/New Testament
Romans 3:23-26

Hebrews 9:11-14

Jesus Sat Down at the Right Hand of the Father (Hebrews 1:3)

5. Look at the following passages and record what you learn about the authority of Jesus Christ and what it means that He sits at the right hand of the Father's throne.

a. Prophetic Word/Old Testament
Psalm 110:1-3

b. God speaking through His Son/New Testament
Mark 16:19

Romans 8:34

Reflect & Respond

Stand in awe of His greatness! From eternity past to eternity future, God is in control. His purpose and plans cannot and will not be thwarted. He is the King of kings and Lord of lords, and one day every knee will bow and every tongue will confess this marvelous truth.

I try to take a Bible with me everywhere I go, because I often have to wait—for the doctor or dentist, an appointment or a friend, or sitting under the dryer at the salon. These are great opportunities to memorize Scripture. Sometimes the whole Bible is too much to carry—write out a verse or two on a three-by-five card and stick it in your wallet. Or use a sticky note and put it on your dashboard or bathroom mirror. Review it in your mind and say it aloud throughout the day. It's so encouraging when the Holy Spirit brings memorized verses to mind at a moment when we need a boost the most.

ⓒ Memorize Hebrews 1:1-4. This is a great passage to memorize, because it exalts Jesus Christ and reminds us that God reaches out to us through a relationship.

DAY FIVE

Reflection

Day Five is a good day to catch up on the week's lesson as well as reflect on what you've observed and gained from your study of the passage. I will provide a few different ways to respond.

I encourage you to write down the things He's showing you, challenging you with, or prodding you on. Keep a record of His work in and through your heart. Record verses or passages that He uses in your life. Keep track of your questions and the answers to your questions.

1.   Conclude your study of Hebrews 1:1-4 by reading the passage aloud and thanking the Lord for each of the significant truths about Christ listed. Thank Him for how they pertain to you individually and to the world as a whole.

2.   I mentioned this in Day Four, and I will again. Our Savior is awesome, isn't He? So that, at any given moment throughout your day you can bring to mind these things that are true of Him, memorize Hebrews 1:1-4.

> ### Memorize Scripture
>
> The best way to have these truths ready to dwell on is by memorizing specific verses and passages. Write each passage on a three-by-five card card and post it on your bathroom mirror or your car's dashboard. Quote it over and over throughout your day, and practice saying it aloud without looking. It takes time, discipline, and work, but the reward is worth the effort.

Throughout the ages, mankind the world over has either hated and despised Jesus Christ and lives in apathetic indifference or active defiance. Some create their own gods and religious belief systems. Many who encounter the living God and recognize their sin and desperate need for a Savior fall on their faces, worship, and give every ounce of their being to serving, honoring, and glorifying Jesus Christ. Others respond halfway, and Christianity becomes nothing more than once-a-week visit to church.

3.   If you had the opportunity to tell someone about Jesus, based upon your personal experience as well as what you've learned from this passage, what would you say?

4. One pastor, after studying this passage and teaching from it, said, "How can we not fall before the Lord and proclaim, 'I will do whatever You ask and follow wherever You lead?'" Why do you think this passage evokes that kind of a response?

5. How are you inclined to respond to the Lord after looking at this passage?

6. In the midst of studying Hebrews 1:1-3 today, I turned to Psalm 22. It's such a beautiful picture of the great awesomeness of our God, so I thought I'd share it with you. As you finish up today, read it aloud to the Lord and praise Him for who He is.

    You who fear the LORD, praise Him;
    All you descendants of Jacob, glorify Him,
    And stand in awe of Him, all you descendants of Israel.
    For He has not despised nor abhorred the affliction of the afflicted;
    Neither has He hidden His face from him;
    But when he cried to Him for help, He heard…
    All the ends of the earth will remember and turn to the LORD,
    And all the families of the nations will worship before You.
    For the kingdom is the LORD's,
    And He rules over the nations.
    (Psalm 22:22-24, 27-28 NASB)

For Further Study

We've looked at Jesus as Creator in this week's lesson, and because we're surrounded by His creation, I wanted to include some more passages for you to ponder.

The following verses show us how God is the ruler over creation and describe His handiwork. Read these and write down any that peak your interest.

- Job 38:8-18 (for a bigger view of God and creation see: Job 37:14-39:30)

- Psalm 104:5-9

- Isaiah 40:18-22

How does the fact that God is the creator of everything encourage you in your present circumstances?

1 John Piper, *Seeing and Savoring Jesus Christ*. Wheaton: Crossway, 2004. page, 15

2 Tom Wright, (*Hebrews for Everyone*. London: Ashford Colour Press, 2003) p. 12.

3 Ibid, page 14.

Jesus, Our Champion

Hebrews 1:4-2:18

The beauty of our Savior never ceases to amaze me even though I've read Hebrews 1:1-4 many times. He is the Son of God, Heir of all things, Creator of the world, and the Radiance of God's glory and exact representation of His nature. He upholds all things by the word of His power and now sits at the right hand of the Majesty on high because He made purification of sins. Everything from eternity past, present, and future is summed up in Jesus Christ. Wow, what a Savior!

The writer of Hebrews begins by exalting Jesus Christ and underlining the fact that He is superior to everything that ever was, is, and ever will be. *The Jewish scriptures [Old Testament] are continually pointing beyond themselves to a further reality which they do no themselves contain. More particularly, they are pointing to a great act of salvation, of dealing with sin, which they do not themselves offer. This great act has now been accomplished in Jesus....* [1] As we continue our look at the superiority of Jesus, we'll begin to see His superiority over all the things that were foundational to the Jewish faith. This week's lesson focuses on how He is superior to angels because Jews had a tendency to elevate and even worship angels. The writer seeks to emphasize that God calls Jesus Son and crowns Him King, while angels are created beings sent to serve and worship Him. We'll see that Jesus, because of His suffering and death, is also champion of our salvation; and because He was made like "us" in all things (He was fully God and fully man), He became our merciful and faithful High Priest.

Take a moment to praise Him for who He is. Thank Him for ways that He manifested Himself and His goodness to you this week. If you had a frustrating week and feel distant from the Lord, then lay all your needs at His feet before you dig into Hebrews. Then, ask His Spirit to use today's study to help you and give you wisdom as you open the Word. Ask Him to give you eyes to see and ears to hear His truth.

DAY ONE

☐ Read Hebrews

Hebrews 1:4-14

"Man is a wonderful and amazing creation—certainly higher than the plants and the animals, even the most complex animals. He is higher than any other material creation. But there are created being even higher than man—the angels. Hebrews 2:9 tells us that when Jesus became a man He was 'made for a little while lower than the angels.' They are holy, powerful, and wise. They do not have the infirmities that men have. They are specially created spirit beings, made by God before He made man. They were, in fact, watching in the heavens when God created the world. They were of a higher order than man, at least higher than fallen man.

The Bible speaks a great deal of angels. There are 108 direct references to angels in the Old Testament and 165 in the New. The primary purpose of their creation was to render special worship and service to God." [2]

A study of angels is intriguing to say the least. Imagine if we were able to see this great heavenly host! This Jewish audience, because of their history, knew a lot about angels, and some Jews even worshiped them. Angels were present at the giving of the Law in the Old Testament and numerous other places, as well. The author of Hebrews seeks to remind the reader, on every level, there is no comparison between Jesus Christ and the angels. In fact, we'll discover their primary purpose is to worship God and serve those who inherit salvation.

Before you begin this week's study, I'd encourage you to pray. Ask the Holy Spirit for wisdom and guidance as you open the Word. Pray that you'll see Jesus in a whole new light as you dig into Hebrews today.

1. Read Hebrews 1:4-14. It is important and fascinating to recognize that angels are real, created beings used by God in many ways throughout the Bible—and in our lives today. Read the following verses and record what you learn about angels:

   a. Hebrews 1:14; 13:2

   b. Psalm 34:7; 91:11

c. Psalm 103:20-21; Revelation 5:11-13 *(Note: "hosts" and "myriads" mean there are too many angels to count.)*

2. Several places in Scripture we're introduced to specific angels in the Lord's service, and I've included a few for our consideration. Look at the verses below and write down what you discover about these angels.

a. Luke 1:8-20, 26-38

b. Jude 9; Revelation 12:10

c John 20:11-12

3.   The Bible teaches us there are also fallen angels, the chief of which is Lucifer—Satan. The following passages provide insight regarding these fallen angels. Read and write down what you discover.

   Isaiah 14:12-14

   Jude 6-7

4.   Look closely at Hebrews 1:4-14 and compare what you learn about Jesus with what you learn about angels. Note that the writer quotes from various prophetic Psalms that look ahead to Jesus as King and Ruler over all:

   <u>Jesus</u>   <u>Angels</u>

5.   Based upon what you've discovered, why is Jesus Christ superior to the angels?

6.   Like the Jewish believers, we need to be reminded that Jesus is worthy of our worship, adoration, and praise. We need to remember more regularly that He is King and Lord, Creator and God. What does it mean to you personally to know that Jesus Christ reached out to you through the Gospel?

Reflect & Respond

In just a few verses, we're reminded that His throne is eternal and His rule is righteous. He laid the foundation of the earth and designed the heavens with His hand. He never, ever changes; therefore, the angels were created by Him for a purpose, the greatest purpose—to worship Him. What a Savior and God we serve! There is nobody like Jesus.

◎ Take some time to worship Him and read Hebrews 1:4-14 aloud. Thank Him for ways you've experienced His creation—enjoying a beautiful sunset or listening to the pounding waves of the ocean. Thank Him for His unchanging character—His love never changes, He is always righteous and good.

◎ Bring Him into your daily life and praise Him for the relationship He initiated with you. He in His great majesty is real and true and personal. He bends down and listens. He hears all of our prayers. Leave none of your concerns uncovered. Lay them all at His feet.

DAY TWO

☐ Read Hebrews

Hebrews 2:1-2

It is believed, because of the content of this letter, the recipients were mostly Jewish believers living in and around Rome. Also, due to the various warnings throughout, it seems as though there were unbelievers in the mix who had yet to make a firm decision to follow Christ. On the heels of the glorious majesty of the Lord Jesus, the writer pauses to exhort and warn the readers to pay much closer attention to what they've heard. In my mind's eye, I picture a large group of people gathered together to listen to this letter. I imagine a group of men and women gathered around a table, leaning in close to hear this exhortation. At the same time, I imagine a few skeptics, stepping back, unsure of what they've heard and not fully convinced that anything can replace the Law and Moses.

Whether you're leaning in closer or unsure about Jesus, ask Him to help you pay much closer attention to what you've heard so far. Pray His Spirit will guide and teach you as you continue.

1. Hebrews 2:1 is the first warning to the readers of this letter: "For this reason we must listen very carefully to the truth we have heard…." According to this verse what will happen if we don't listen carefully (keep your eyes on the text)?

2. Use a dictionary or www.dictionary.com and define *drift*.

3.   a. After reading and studying the great truths of Chapter One, why do you think there's potential to drift and lose sight of the great majesty of our Lord Jesus?

b. What might it look like to drift away from what we've heard?

Truth Search

Biblical commentator John MacArthur provides this insight into angels and the Ten Commandments, *"Why is the Old Testament law, particularly the Ten Commandments, so connected with angels? Why does the writer emphasize that angels mediated the Old Covenant? He does so because the angels were instrumental in bringing the Ten Commandments…."* [3] MacArthur refers to Psalm 68:17, Deuteronomy 33:2, and Acts 7:53 as verses that indicate the presence of myriads of angels present at the giving of the Law.

However, regardless of their presence and the size of their armies, angels pale in comparison to Jesus Christ, Savior and Son of God.

4.   Hebrews 2:2 says, *"For if the message spoken through angels was binding, and every violation and disobedience received its just punishment, how will we escape if we ignore such a great salvation?"*

a. Look closely at the text. What is the consequence of every violation and disobedience according to the Law?

b. For further insight look at Romans 3:19-23 and Galatians 3:10. Record what more you learn about the Law and consequences of sin.

5. The writer goes on to describe salvation as "great" and warns against "ignoring" it.

a. According to the following, what makes this salvation great and greater than the Law? Hebrews 1:3; 10:12-14

Romans 3:24-26

Galatians 3:12-14

b. Based upon what you've learned, is there any other way to escape the consequences of "every violation and disobedience" apart from this great salvation?

c. There are many people who hear the gospel over and over again and still reject it. Why are they warned against ignoring it?

Matthew Henry, who lived and died in the 18th century, is one of my favorite biblical commentators. He writes this about our salvation:

*"It is a great salvation that the gospel discovers, for it **discovers a great Saviour**, one who has manifested God to be reconciled to our nature, and reconcilable to our persons; it shows how we may be saved from such great sin and such great misery, and be restored to such great holiness and such great happiness."* [4] (Emphasis added)

This great salvation was first spoken through the Lord Himself and confirmed by those who heard it from Him. Then it was confirmed by signs and wonders, various miracles, and gifts of the Holy Spirit, which is evidenced all the way through the book of Acts. In fact, the power of the Gospel is evidenced in all of our lives—Jesus Christ transforms, changes, and conforms us to His image. The transformation and changes are evidence of the power of the Gospel at work in us individually and in us as a Christian community.

7. a. In what ways have you experienced the transforming work of the Holy Spirit in your life. What changes has He made in your character, priorities, etc.? You might look back to the beginning of your Christian life, which for some might be years and years back, but don't sidestep looking for changes that are apparent right now, since our relationship is living and dynamic, changing and growing.

b. Do you feel like you're drifting or simply at a standstill? This would be a great time to talk to the Lord about your spiritual condition. You obviously want Jesus to take first place in your heart, or you'd be doing something else with your time. Sometimes when I feel lethargic or stuck, I'll go back to the early days when I placed my faith in Christ. I'll reflect on what I was thinking back then, how little I knew the Bible, how unfamiliar Jesus was to me, and how terribly little I knew about His Spirit. I'll also remember the many, many ways He protected me and kept me walking toward Him.

Reflect & Respond

What might tempt you to drift away from what you know about Jesus rather than pay much closer attention? If you're anything like me, it could be distractions like a cell phone or the Internet, the latest sale at the mall, or something really mindless on television. Or, it could be good things like serving the Lord, doing our jobs, and helping other people in our families or community. It doesn't take much to take our attention off of Jesus.

Do you ever feel you want to stand firm and steady, but you're not very sure-footed? Over the years I've become increasingly aware of the fact that I am weak and need the Spirit's power to help me read my Bible without being distracted by what I'm going to wear to work or fix for dinner. I need Him to help me maintain perspective when things aren't going very well. This portion of Psalm 103 reassures us that yes, we're weak, but God is not.

Psalm 103:14-17 says, *"Just as a father has compassion on his children, so the* LORD *has compassion on those who fear Him. For He Himself knows our frame (what we are made of); He is mindful that we are but dust. As for man, his days are like grass; as a flower of the field, so he flourishes. When the wind has passed over it, it is no more; and its place acknowledges it no longer. But the lovingkindness of the* LORD *is from everlasting to everlasting on those how fear Him, and His righteousness, to children's children."*

℮   If this strikes a chord, talk to the Lord and admit you need Him to keep you from drifting. Ask Him to give you the strength to pay close attention to Him.

℮   Perhaps you're doing this study and you've heard the Gospel a number of times but have yet to place your faith in Christ. What is keeping you from receiving this great gift of salvation? Let me encourage you to respond to the Lord today—listen to His song of love and salvation. Meditate on the beautiful truth of Christ's love that He demonstrated at the cross. He will help you in your unbelief—all you need to do is ask.

DAY THREE

Digging Deeper

I love Psalm 102 because the writer, in the midst of pain and affliction, expressed himself so honestly before the Lord. Woven throughout this prayer is a raw honesty mingled with words of faith and trust. The great and awesome God described in Hebrews chapter one is the One who is intimately acquainted with all of our ways and involved in our daily lives.

Pray for a soft and teachable heart as you open the Word today.

1. Begin by reading all of Psalm 102.

¹ Hear my prayer, O Lord;
let my cry for help come to you.
² Do not hide your face from me
when I am in distress.
Turn your ear to me;
when I call, answer me quickly.
³ For my days vanish like smoke;
my bones burn like glowing embers.
⁴ My heart is blighted and withered like grass;
I forget to eat my food.
⁵ Because of my loud groaning
I am reduced to skin and bones.
⁶ I am like a desert owl,
like an owl among the ruins.
⁷ I lie awake; I have become
like a bird alone on a roof.
⁸ All day long my enemies taunt me;
those who rail against me use my name as a curse.
⁹ For I eat ashes as my food
and mingle my drink with tears
¹⁰ because of your great wrath,
for you have taken me up and thrown me aside.
¹¹ My days are like the evening shadow;
I wither away like grass.
¹² But you, O Lord, sit enthroned forever;
your renown endures through all generations.

¹³ You will arise and have compassion on Zion,
for it is time to show favor to her;
the appointed time has come.
¹⁴ For her stones are dear to your servants;
her very dust moves them to pity.
¹⁵ The nations will fear the name of the LORD,
all the kings of the earth will revere your glory.
¹⁶ For the LORD will rebuild Zion
and appear in his glory.
¹⁷ He will respond to the prayer of the destitute;
he will not despise their plea.
¹⁸ Let this be written for a future generation,
that a people not yet created may praise the LORD :
¹⁹ "The LORD looked down from his sanctuary on high,
from heaven he viewed the earth,
²⁰ to hear the groans of the prisoners
and release those condemned to death."
²¹ So the name of the LORD will be declared in Zion
and his praise in Jerusalem
²² when the peoples and the kingdoms
assemble to worship the LORD.
²³ In the course of my life he broke my strength;
he cut short my days.
²⁴ So I said:
"Do not take me away, O my God, in the midst of my days;
your years go on through all generations.
²⁵ In the beginning you laid the foundations of the earth,
and the heavens are the work of your hands.
²⁶ They will perish, but you remain;
they will all wear out like a garment.
Like clothing you will change them
and they will be discarded.
²⁷ But you remain the same,
and your years will never end.
²⁸ The children of your servants will live in your presence;
their descendants will be established before you" (NIV).

2. Look closely at Psalm 102:1-11. How does the writer describe his circumstances, and how would you describe his emotional state and his relationship with God? Be specific.

3. What does the psalmist request of God (there are several things)?

I love the Psalms because they've taught me so much about relating to the Lord. I love how the writer of this Psalm honestly and bluntly shares his feelings and perspective. He didn't hide his emotion from the Lord or try to say the "right" or most "spiritual" things to the Lord; instead, he laid it all out for Him to see.

4. Describe a time when you felt like the psalmist.

5. The writer continues his prayer to the Lord in Psalm 102:12-17.

   a. How does his perspective change and what's his focus?

b. What about God does the psalmist take comfort in according to Psalm 102:12-17?

c. Why is it important in the midst of loneliness, depression, rejection, fear, or the spiritual battle to recognize the truth about God?

6. a. Continue reading Psalm 102:18-22. Record what you learn about the Lord; then, record what you learn about His role in your life.

b. What's the ultimate result of God's grace according to this portion of the Psalm?

7. Finally, consider Psalm 102:23-28. Write down what you discover about God compared to His creation and created beings.

Reflect & Respond

Sometimes in the midst of life's complexities we lose sight of the fact that God is with us. We listen to the world's perspective on television or the radio that offers temporary and self-centered solutions to our problems—usually we're told we need to lose weight or make more money. Satan also whispers lies about God's character and tries to tell us that God doesn't care, our problems are too small, and our lack of faith thwarts His love and attention. The truth is, He's on our side. Nothing about God or His character, His plan, or His purpose ever changes. We're often tempted to look elsewhere for help and hope, and that's when we need the Lord the most.

◎ Maybe you're facing similar challenges as the writer of Psalm 102. What lies are you tempted to believe about God and what truths have you looked at today that have reassured you or have given you courage?

◎ This week, every time you're tempted to look at your circumstances or to believe something that's not true about the Lord, go back to the truth of God's character revealed in His Word. *"Lord, I feel lonely and forgotten. I don't know where to turn. You seem so far away, and it feels like You don't care about me. I want to believe that You hear my groaning; You know my situation. I need help and comfort."*

DAY FOUR

☐ Read Hebrews

Hebrews 2:4-18

As we continue to discover more about the superiority of Jesus, the author of Hebrews hones in on the significant fact that Jesus was both fully God and fully man. In a great book about the beauty of Jesus and our salvation called *Going Deeper*, J. Sidlow Baxter writes, "He was, as he evermore is, the eternal Son of God, and God the Son, but He was not the Son of Man until He was born of Mary. He has now become Man by a real human birth; He has lived our life, and shared our lot, and undergone our temptations, and borne our griefs, and died our death; and He has risen again, still the same Jesus, for He is 'Jesus Christ the same yesterday and today and to the ages' (Hebrews 13:8). His human nature (Marvel again at the miracle and mystery of it!) is now blended forever with His deity; and he is now omnipresently with all his people everywhere, and with each of us, as the ever-living, ever-loving Lord JESUS." [5]

"Open my eyes that I may behold wonderful things from Your Word" (Psalm 119:18). Oh that the Lord might open our eyes wide to the rich truths of who He is as we dig into His Word today.

1. Examine Hebrews 2:5-10, 16-18 and record two or more things you learn about:
    • Angels

    • Man

    • Jesus

It's interesting to note that Hebrews 2:5-8 tells us that God subjected all things to mankind, and not to angels. However, it has not been man's experience to rule all things. One day it will be true, but until then, we have Jesus who does rule over all things. His victory over sin and death confirms His Majesty and sovereign control. Ray Stedman, pastor of Peninsula Bible Church and biblical commentator, writes the following, "Our intended destiny was one of power and authority over all the conditions and life of earth. If this was our commission from the moment of creation, what light it sheds on our responsibility to care for this planet and its creatures! We were not given dominion so the earth and the animals should serve us; rather, we are given authority to develop them to the fullest extent intended by the fruitful mind of the Creator. We are to serve them by thorough knowledge and loving care, in the form of servant-leadership which the Lord himself manifested when he came.

Yet, says this writer in what must be the understatement of the ages, we do not see everything subject to him. No, there are many things fallen humans cannot control: the weather, the seasons, the instincts of animals, the tides, our own passions, international events, natural disasters, and on and on. The increasing pollution of the planet, the spread of famines and wars, the toll taken by drugs, accidents and disease, all tell the story of a lost destiny.

But almost with a shout the author cries, but we see Jesus! He is the last hope of a dying race. And that hope lies both in his deity and his humanity. He alone, as a human being, managed to fulfill what was intended for us from the beginning." [6]

2. Look again at Hebrews 2:5-10 and record the result of Christ's suffering and death, and then add to the list of Hebrews 1:3.

Contemporary pastor and author John Piper writes in his book *Seeing and Savoring Jesus Christ*:

"This is the consistent teaching of the Bible. Christ was sinless. Although he was the divine Son of God, he was really human, with all our temptations and appetites and physical weaknesses…Therefore, when the Bible says that Jesus 'learned obedience through what he suffered,' it doesn't mean that he learned to stop disobeying. It means that with each new trial he learned in practice—and in pain—what it means to obey. When it says that he was 'made perfect through suffering,' it doesn't mean that he was gradually getting rid of defects. It means that he was gradually fulfilling the perfect righteousness that he had to have in order to save us." [7]

3. Hebrews 2:11-18 explains the extent to which Jesus went on our behalf so that we are now called His "brethren" and His "children." Observe each verse and write down what you discover about Jesus and the result of His actions:

    Hebrews 2:11-13

    Hebrews 2:14-15

    Hebrews 2:16-18

Truth Search

4. Jesus became of flesh and blood in order to render the devil powerless. Take a look at the following verses and record what you learn about Satan/devil:

    Revelation 12:9; 20:2-3, 10

    II Corinthians 11:3

    John 8:44

5. Satan is the accuser of the brethren (Revelation 12:10) and at the same time the Father of all liars. We're so prone to listen to his accusations and forget the pure and beautiful truth of the Gospel. Some of Satan's most common lies go like this:

    "He will never forgive that sin."
    "You did that again? You can't ask for forgiveness. You've asked too many times."
    "Everything about you is unlovable. How do you expect God to love you?"
    "You're guilty, guilty, guilty!"
    "One more time won't matter."

    What are some of Satan's lies you hear and believe?

6. Based upon what you've learned about Jesus in just a few chapters, what are some of the truths you can count on?

7. Glance one more time at Hebrews 2:9-18. Look for all of the words that describe Christ and His gift of salvation. For example:

Hebrews 2:9—He tasted death for everyone

Hebrews 2:10—God perfected Him through suffering

Hebrews 2:11—He is not ashamed to call them brethren

Reflect & Respond

Proclaim His name and sing His praise because He is worthy. Thank Him for tasting death for you so you might live eternally. Thank Him for suffering and enduring the cross for you and what this means as you go about your day. Unlike Jesus, we're not perfect. We're fallen creatures who need a Savior—not just once—but every single day. He is the eternal champion of our salvation—the King of kings and Lord of lords, and He's also very present inside us at every single moment. He lives in us and empowers us with His Spirit. Rejoice that you have a relationship with Him.

DAY FIVE

We have covered a lot of ground this week and uncovered truth that is foundational to our lives both now and into eternity. Most of all, Jesus Christ continues to come to the forefront. He is our matchless Savior—there is nobody like Him. He is sovereign over all creation and controls all things by the Word of His power. I take comfort in these truths as gas prices continue to rise and the stock market falls yet again. From an earthly standpoint, nothing is stable or secure. But from a heavenly view, He is absolutely in control. I'm so thankful for Him.

1. So, if you're behind in the lesson, take time to catch up today.

2. Whether you're finished or not, review what we've covered and uncovered. You might want to go back to those truths that are new to you and write them down or reread the passages of scripture that struck you this week.

3. Bring the Lord into your daily experience by reflecting again on Psalm 102. For example, if you're troubled by the current economic news or world events, read Psalm 102:12-17 out loud. Acknowledge your eternal and sovereign God along with His compassion, grace, and tenderness.

4. I love being reminded that Jesus initiated a personal relationship with me, and He calls me His child and His sister. Amazing! As you contemplate your relationship with Him, write out a prayer and express your gratitude, ask questions, and tell Him what you're learning and how you want to grow. Include verses or thoughts from this week's lesson, if you want to.

For Further Study

Jesus Christ is victorious over sin and death, which is why we call Him our Champion. He conquered sin and death and rendered Satan powerless.

- Look at the following and write down what you learn about our Champion:
  I Corinthians 15:54-58

  II Timothy 1:10

  Revelation 19:11-16 (this describes Jesus at His second coming)

- How can the truth about your Champion make a difference today in your life?

1 John MacArthur, *The MacArthur New Testament Commentary HEBREWS*, (Chicago, Moody Press, 1983), p.

2 John MacArthur, *The MacArthur New Testament Commentary HEBREWS* (Chicago, Moody Press, 1983), p. 22

3 John MacArthur, *The MacArthur New Testament Commentary HEBREWS* (Chicago, Moody Press, 1983), p.46

4 Matthew Henry, *Commentary On the Whole Bible* (Hendrickson Online Publishing, 1991,1994)

5 J. Sidlow Baxter, *Going Deeper* (Zondervan, Chicago, 1959), p. 19.

6 Ray Stedman, *Sermons on Hebrews* (Online Commentary), p.14.

7 John Piper, *Seeing and Savoring Jesus Christ* (Crossway, Wheaton. 2004), pp. 24-25.

Jesus, God's Faithful Son

Hebrews 3:1-16

Do you ever feel that God will like you better, answer your prayers more fully, allow things to go more smoothly, or minimize difficulties if you read your Bible regularly, attend church weekly, pray consistently before every meal, and stay away from R-rated movies? Just this week, I found myself hesitating to pray. My time in the Word hadn't been what I thought it should be, so I figured I'd lost some of my privileges as God's child. Sometimes, when the world's problems seem especially demanding, I'm tempted to feel like my life is of little consequence to God, so I attempt to deal with my seemingly minor problems on my own. Then I remember, this isn't a religion but a relationship—a secure relationship based on Christ's work on the cross, not my work for Christ. It's also a relationship where God wants me to depend upon and take refuge in Him.

The Jewish believers who received this letter were experiencing tough circumstances. They were being persecuted for their faith, and they were discouraged and tempted—tempted to drift, harden their hearts, and depreciate the salvation found only in Jesus Christ. The writer of this letter takes great care to exalt Christ to His rightful position—King, Creator, and Eternal God—higher than the angels. He reminds the audience that Jesus was crowned with glory and honor because He took on flesh, was made like his brethren in all things, and suffered and died for everyone. Only Jesus could make purification for sin because He is fully God and fully man. Only Jesus could render the devil powerless, deliver those who are slaves to sin, and satisfy the wrath of God against sin—He is fully God and fully man—all things neither angels nor the Law could accomplish.

In addition, Jesus is better than Moses. John MacArthur (pastor of Grace Community Church and another of my favorite biblical commentators) remind us, "Moses was esteemed by the Jews far above any other Jew who ever lived…He was the man to whom God spoke face to face, through whom He performed miracle after miracle. He had seen the very glory of God…Some Jews believed that Moses was greater than angels. God spoke to the prophets in visions, but to Moses He spoke face to face." [1]

The Gospel story is all about Jesus—from beginning to end. It's not about angels, laws or rituals, the devil, or Moses. Everything pales in comparison to our Savior Jesus Christ.

Today, as you crack open your Bible to the book of Hebrews, pour yourself a cup of your favorite beverage (I prefer black coffee.) and find a comfortable place to sit and enjoy your time with Jesus. Take in God's truth, and let it wash over your heart and soul. It's my prayer we'll all find ourselves drawn to Jesus in a fresh way.

DAY ONE

☐ Read Hebrews

Hebrews 3:1-6

1. Read Hebrews 3:1-6.

2. Note Hebrews 3:1 begins with "therefore," which connects the previous passage with the one to come. Whenever you see the word "therefore," ask yourself the question, "What is the 'therefore' there for?" Therefore, consider Jesus in light of the fact that He tasted death for everyone and sanctified us (made us holy), because He rendered the devil powerless, delivered us from the fear of death, and comes to our aid when we're tempted.

    Use a dictionary or www.dictionary.com and define *consider:*

Truth Search

3. The writer of Hebrews highlights two roles of Jesus to consider: Apostle (or "sent one") and High Priest, which Hebrews 4-8 covers extensively. In the Gospel of John (one of my favorite gospels), Jesus refers over and over again to the fact He's sent from God. So, to enhance our study, we're going to spend a little time in the Gospel of John.

    a. Look at the following passages and record what you learn about the Sent One.
       John 3:31-34

       John 5:30-38

John 6:30-38

John 17:1-3; 7-8

John 17: 18-23

Earlier this week, the temptation to believe that I had somehow disappointed God, and therefore wasn't worthy to enter into His presence, resulted from listening to whispers from the Evil One, who speaks lies that sound so true! It's in those very moments we need to stop and consider Jesus—to fix our eyes on Him and remember who He is. A speaker I once heard said we need to "practice the presence of God." This makes a lot of sense, doesn't it?

When Satan's whispers begin to scream or I face temptation, it helps me to "walk through" Philippians 4:8-9, which also is a great passage to memorize. It's amazing. Once I begin to replace the lies with the truth of Jesus and His Word, I experience great peace and perspective. So, here's what I do. It's simple, but it really helps me take the focus off of me and put it back on Christ.

First, I'll write down the lie or temptation in my journal. Then, I'll write out Philippians 4:8.

Finally brethren whatever is true—What is true of the Lord? What is true of me? What is true of the situation? I'll look through Scripture passages like Romans 5:1-9, Ephesians 1:3-14, and Colossians 1:3-9 and write specific verses in my journal.

Whatever is right—Sometimes I repeat what I wrote above; other times I distinguish between "right and wrong."

Whatever is pure—Often Jesus is the only thing that's pure about a lie or temptation—so, I'll look at Him.

Whatever is lovely—What lovely things come to your mind? Read Psalm 84:1-4 and Isaiah 52:7 for some ideas.

Whatever is of good repute (this speaks of good character or reputation)—Think through godly character and use Jesus as your example. Look at passages like John 4:1-10 to see how Jesus interacted with a woman drawing water from a well. Read Luke 4:16-22 and think about how people described Jesus.

If there is any excellence—Define the word excellence. Does your mind dwell on excellent things?

Anything worthy of praise—Who is worthy of praise and why?

Let your mind dwell on these things—To dwell means "to live and have a home in a particular place." When our minds reside in God's truth, we experience the peace the surpasses comprehension (Philippians 4:7,9) because we're dwelling on Jesus Christ and not ourselves. Usually I get halfway through this list and whatever was plaguing my mind disappears because I'm replacing those thoughts with the Lord Jesus.

5.   Hebrews 3:1 tells us we're holy partakers of a heavenly calling. Look up the following passages and record what you learn about this heavenly calling:

Philippians 3:14, 20

I Peter 2:9-10

"It is a heavenly calling because it comes from heaven—from God. And it is a heavenly calling because it invites us and leads us to heaven—to God. In other words, this 'heavenly calling' relates to the two great needs that we have: a word from God and a way to God. It's a heavenly calling, which means it is a word from heaven, a word from God. And it's a calling, which means it is meant to show us the way home to God. Christians are people who have been gripped by this calling. The word of God broke through our resistance, and took hold of us with the truth and love of Christ, and reconciled us to God and is now leading us home to heaven." [2]

6.   You and I are called with a "heavenly calling," and our purpose is to bring honor and glory to Jesus Christ, to take part in building His kingdom. What does this mean for you as a student or a mom, a child or a parent, an executive or a coffee barista?

Reflect & Respond

Jesus Christ is the centerpiece of everything we believe. He is the Sent One and the way to God. He is the Messenger and the Message. He is the Word from God and the way home to God. It's so important we "consider" or "fix our thoughts" on Jesus so we don't drift away from what we've heard. It's tempting to look at our circumstances and forget God's involved, intimately, with our lives. There's so much more going on than what meets the eye.

- ☺ Reflect on your life at present. What are you involved in day to day? Think about particular circumstances or relationships, at work, in class, etc. Maybe like the recipients of this letter, you're in the midst of a really hard time and you're disillusioned. It could be you don't really think about Jesus that much, and He's not really a very big part of your life. Do you ever feel tempted to think you need something or someone other than Jesus? Is following Him really the best option?

What do you tend to "fix your thoughts on" in the midst of these circumstances? Where does your mind tend to go? Whatever you might be feeling or thinking, write it down and talk to the Lord about it.

- ☺ Then "consider" this same situation, only color it with the fact that you're a holy partaker of a heavenly calling. Does your life reflect this call? Describe how you feel and what comes to mind.

- ☺ The writer of Hebrews continually reminds us to "consider" Jesus because, like believers down through the ages, we need to remember who He is and why we're here. Read the following passage aloud and make it a prayer for your life today.

> *Keep your eyes on Jesus, who both began and finished this race we're in. Study how he did it. Because he never lost sight of where he was headed—that exhilarating finish in and with God—he could put up with anything along the way: cross, shame, whatever. And now he's there, in the place of honor, right alongside God. When you find yourselves flagging in your faith, go over that story again, item by item, that long litany of hostility he plowed through. That will shoot adrenaline into your souls! (Hebrews 12:2-3, The Message)*

DAY TWO

☐ Read Hebrews

Hebrews 3:2-6

As believers (holy partakers of a heavenly calling), we're reminded to contemplate, fix our gaze, think seriously about, and consider Jesus the Apostle and High Priest of our confession. As we look at Hebrews 3:2-6, the faithfulness of Christ is highlighted and compared with an Old Testament prototype—Moses.

Remember that the audience who received this letter considered Moses an extremely important figure in their history. He delivered the Israelites from slavery, defeated Pharaoh, and received the Law directly from God. Exodus 33:11 reveals the special relationship God had with Moses. "Thus the LORD used to speak to Moses face to face, just as a man speaks to his friend." For those who wavered and wondered if Jesus Christ truly was superior, they had to contend with the difference between Him and Moses. Yes, Moses was greatly used by God as a servant, but he can't compare with Jesus, who was God's Son.

1. Read Hebrews 3:2-4. Why was Jesus counted worthy of more glory than Moses?

2. What, according to Hebrews 3:5-6, was Moses' role in God's house and for what purpose?

3. What was Jesus' role in God's house (Look closely at Hebrews 3:3, 4, 6.)?

Harry Ironside is another favorite biblical commentator. He served the Lord for 50 years as an American Bible teacher, a pastor of The Moody Church for a season, and an author of many articles and pamphlets. His series of straightforward, biblical commentaries has encouraged me and given me insight into God's Word for a long time. He writes this about Hebrews 3:3-6: "He [Jesus] is infinitely superior to Moses because Moses, though faithful in his day, was simply a servant in the house of God, but Christ Jesus is the Builder of the house and is Son over His own house, whose house we are, if we hold fast the confidence and the rejoicing of the hope firm unto the end. Observe that the term 'house' is used here in three senses. The house in which Moses was faithful was the tabernacle. But the tabernacle was the pattern of things in the heavens…. But the house over which Christ is set and to which we belong is that building composed of living stones in which every believer has a place." [3]

Truth Search

4. As you look at this passage closely, it says that "Christ was faithful as a Son over His house whose house we are…."

    a. For insight into Christ's house, look at the following passages and record what you learn:
    I Corinthians 3:16-17

    Ephesians 2:19-21

    I Peter 2:5

    b. This is an awesome and incomprehensible thought. The Spirit of God lives in me. I am His home, and so are you, if you're His child. What are the implications of this truth for you and for all believers?

Reflect & Respond

The more I look at Hebrews the more I marvel at God's eternal plan and purpose. Everything is summed up in Christ—everything. The more I realize this fact, the more I understand why the writer of this letter exhorts us to not drift away or neglect our salvation. My need to "consider Jesus" seems more apparent to me as I study. It's so easy along the journey of life to forget about the eternal purpose of God and the glory of Christ.

- Diligence looks different depending upon what stage of life we're in. When I first began to learn about Jesus and the Bible, I knew absolutely nothing about either. The Bible was dry and uninteresting until I began to read it. Then, it became confusing. Why was there an "Old" and "New" Testament? If the "Old" was old, why did they keep in around? I had no idea where to begin. The Lord brought different people into my life who helped me get started. My friend Kathy, who mentored me when I was in college, explained why it was helpful to read the Bible regularly. She helped me create a plan for reading and then asked me what I was learning.

- If you're just beginning your journey with the Savior, make a daily plan. Set aside time to read and pray. I started by carving out 15 minutes a day, which at the time was extremely difficult. Kathy encouraged me to find a quiet place with the least amount of distractions. So, after I showered and readied myself for the day, I poured myself a cup of coffee and tried to read. Usually I fell asleep, but eventually 15 minutes wasn't long enough anymore.

   Because you're studying Hebrews, start there. Carve out a 15 minute block of time. It might be different each day depending upon your schedule. Do as much of the study as you can, and spend some time in prayer.

- It's possible you've known the Lord for a while, and your time with Him has become stale, or you're just going through the motions. Change your scenery and, if you can, meet with Him somewhere new. Or, freshen up your usual "spot." Approach your time with a sense of anticipation: "Lord, what will I learn about You today?"

DAY THREE

Digging Deeper

Moses, as Hebrews 3:5 says, was "faithful as a servant, for a testimony of those things which were to be spoken later." God gave the Law to Moses and instructed him to build a tabernacle or sanctuary where God's glory would dwell and in which to house the Ark of the Covenant (where the Ten Commandments were stored). In addition, the Lord also commissioned Aaron and his sons to the priesthood. As you read, note the specific detail God gives to Moses as well as the incredible responsibility that was placed upon Moses.

1. According to Exodus 25:8, for what purpose did God instruct Moses to build a tabernacle?

2. Read the following verses, which provide a broad overview of the tabernacle, and write down what you learn.
    Exodus 35:10-19

    Exodus 35:30-36:1

    Exodus 38:24-31

3. Read Exodus 40:1-16. Moses' faithfulness is summed up in verses 16, "Thus Moses did; according to all that the Lord had commanded him, so he did." Continue reading Exodus 40:17-38 and record what more you learn about the Lord and Moses.

Moses was faithful as a servant in God's house. He made sure the tabernacle of God was built according to exact specifications; he appointed the priests just as God instructed. He did everything God commanded him to do—in the face of significant obstacles. But, unlike Jesus, Moses was just a man. And everything that Moses did was a "copy" of what was to come. It was all in God's plan to send His Son, Immanuel (God with us), to dwell in us and not in a house made with hands.

Hebrews 3:6 says, "Jesus was faithful as a Son over His house whose house we are...." It's very mystifying to realize that the Spirit of God lives in us. We are His home. I remember hearing this for the first time, long ago. I don't think I fully understood what it meant, but God helped me grasp, in a small way, that whatever I did and wherever I went, Jesus was there with me. There was great joy and consternation in that realization!

Hebrews 3:6 goes on to say, "...if we hold fast our confidence firm until the end." It's tempting to think "if I hold fast my confidence firm until the end then I'm safe, but if I lose my grip and waver, then I'm in big trouble." This statement means that perseverance, until the end, is evidence of our salvation. There is no doubt that every single one of us will encounter difficulty and challenge along the course of our lives. Trials, temptations, and affliction are used by God to teach us to trust Him and draw us close to Him and deepen our relationship with Him.

Whenever we're tempted to believe we have something to do with our salvation or somehow our good works secure our place in heaven, we need to look back to Jesus Christ. He is superior to the Law, and because of His death, burial, and resurrection, our salvation is secure. He is all we need.

4. How does knowing that Jesus Christ lives in you affect your decisions and choices, your purpose and prayer life?

Reflect & Respond

Hebrews chapter 3 begins with an exhortation to "holy brethren, partakers of a heavenly calling," which is not small or insignificant nor does it take place on a part-time basis. It's serious and eternal business to follow Christ. It takes diligence on our part and a growing understanding of our need to depend upon Jesus.

The Israelites witnessed the awesome power and wonder of God in ways we may never see, and yet they continuously took their eyes off of God and put them onto their circumstances. They were self-centered, hard-hearted, idolatrous sinners. When we put ourselves in their sandals, we do the very same thing. We choose not to find comfort in the fact God's ways are not our ways, His timing is different, and His purposes far outweigh our temporal understanding of things. We often begin looking for solutions that are tangible; we give up and figure God doesn't care anyway; or we look for ways to satisfy our longings and we forget to consider Jesus. He is always with you and me.

◎ Write down three or four ways you've experienced the work of God in your life over the past month. How can these experiences help you as you look to what's ahead?

◎ What is the Lord teaching you about perseverance and hope right now?

DAY FOUR

☐ Read Hebrews

Hebrews 3:12-16

The children of Israel experienced God and His grace and faithfulness in very tangible ways. They were miraculously delivered from the Egyptian plagues and slavery. They walked across the Red Sea on dry land (imagine the walls of water on either side being still just long enough for them to pass). They were led by a great cloud by day and the pillar of fire by night, and the manna and quail were visible reminders of His presence. Yet, their most common response—evidenced by grumbling, disputing, and idolatry—was unbelief. There were some, like Moses and Aaron, Caleb and Joshua, who did believe (although not perfectly) and trusted God's promises. But most experienced God's blessings without ever really knowing Him.

1. Compare Hebrews 3:7-19 with I Corinthians 10:1-13.

    a. How did the Israelites try and test God?

    b. What was the root cause of their sin?

    c. I Corinthians 10:1-3 tells us that although every Israelite experienced God's miraculous deliverance and supernatural provision, not everyone believed in God. In fact, many craved evil things, practiced idolatry and immorality, grumbled against the Lord, and eventually suffered the consequences of unbelief. According to I Corinthians 10:6 and 11, what happened as a result of their sin and why?

2. What exhortations does the writer leave us with in I Corinthians 10:12-14?

"…and God is faithful, who will not allow you to be tempted beyond what you are able, but with the temptation will provide the way of escape also, that you may be able to endure it." The passage is a good reminder that we're all weak and prone to sin. Like the Israelites, it doesn't take much for us to forget the incredible way God provides and protects. We're prone to take our eyes off of Him, which is why we need our Savior every single day. I love this verse because the attention is on God—His faithfulness and His provision. I don't have to "find the strength within myself" to flee temptation. I need to call out to Him in faith—even in desperation. He promises to give me everything I need to escape and endure.

3. Not only does this passage cause me to think about my response to God as I'm faced with temptation, but I also think of several people in my life who have heard the gospel, have experienced God's blessings, and have seen Him work, but their hearts are hard. They refuse to trust in Jesus Christ. Some are very religious and are depending upon their "good works" to get them to heaven; some are convinced they don't need Him; and others call themselves Christians but are unwilling to give up sinful lifestyles as they've been deceived by the passing pleasure of sin. In essence they've turned away from the living God.

I bank on the fact that God wishes none to perish, but for all to come to repentance, and there is still time for my unbelieving friends and family to respond to Christ.

a. Notice how Hebrews 3:7, 13, 15 all refer to "today." Why is there a sense of urgency?

b. How would you describe repentance to someone who doesn't know Christ personally?

Truth Search

5. All of us who know and walk with Jesus will struggle with unbelief throughout our lives. Circumstances look bleak and hopeless at times, and like the children of Israel, we might wonder how we're going to make it through difficult times. I love how the Word reminds us over and over to recognize our need, our helplessness, or our weakness and then turn to Jesus—consider Him.

   a. Look at the following verses and passages and record what you learn.
      Mark 9:17-24

      Hebrews 4:14-16

      James 1:2-5

   b. What looks bleak or hopeless in your life this week? What is going on that makes you wonder if there's light at the end of the tunnel? How has God used His Word to encourage you through your study this week? Or, maybe He seems silent and you wonder if He's hearing your prayers. Either way, journal your thoughts and concerns with the Lord and share them with someone who will pray with and for you.

   c. Finally, in Hebrews 3:12-15, why is it significant that we encourage one another?

Reflect & Respond

I love the fact God loves you and me despite our bouts of unbelief and lack of trust. He is patient with us as we stumble along and always is there to lift us up. He is faithful. He provides escape and power to endure and persevere. Consider Jesus with me—today.

DAY FIVE

☐ Read Hebrews

As you catch up on your reading and this week's lesson, I've included some passages that always inspire me to seek the Lord.

"The steps of a man are established by the LORD; and He delights in his way. When he falls he shall not be hurled headlong; because the LORD is the One who holds His hand" (Psalm 37:23-24).

What a beautiful picture of God's sweet, faithful, loving care and protection. All we need to do is grab hold of His hand. If you've nearly fallen this week, grab hold of His hand and allow Him to pick you up.

"My sheep hear My voice, and I know them, and they follow Me; and I give eternal life to them, and they shall never perish; and no one shall snatch them out of My hand" (John 10:27-28).

Hold fast to this assurance. Pray that the Lord will use the "stuff" in your life to make you attentive and more and more familiar with His voice. Rest in the assurance that no one can snatch you out of His hand.

"Blessed is a man who perseveres under trial; for once he has been approved, he will receive the crown of life which the Lord has promised to those who love Him. Let no one say when he is tempted, 'I am being tempted by God'; for God cannot be tempted by evil, and He Himself does not tempt anyone. But each one is tempted when he is carried away and enticed by his own lust…do not be deceived my beloved brethren" (James 1:12-14, 16).

"No temptation has overtaken you but such as is common to man; and God is faithful, who will not allow you to be tempted beyond what you are able, but with the temptation will provide the way of escape also, that you may be able to endure it" (I Corinthians 10:13).

If temptation and sin lurk at your door, remember to "consider Jesus." Press in close to Him, and ask Him to help you realize afresh why He is the only One who satisfies.

1. Confess your sin (I John 1:9). Confess means to "agree with God about your sin."

2. Call on His faithfulness and power to rescue you from temptation and deception. Philippians 4:13 says, "I can do all things through Christ who strengthens me." Remember the focus is on Jesus and not on your ability or maturity—or lack thereof.

3. Look to your community for encouragement and prayer. Talk to a mentor or a close friend and ask for prayer.

4. Stand firm on His promise. He will provide the way of escape.

---

1 MacArthur, John, *The MacArthur New Testament Commentary HEBREWS* (Chicago, Moody Press, 1983), p. 74.

2 John Piper. *Sermon: Jesus: Worthy of More Glory than Moses.* (1996)

3 H.A. Ironside, *Hebrews-James-Peter.* (American Bible Conference Association, Philadelphia, 1932) p. 55.

Jesus, Our Rest

Hebrews 3:15-4:13

I've decided it takes work to rest. I have to turn off my phone and computer lest they distract me. I have to make a list of all of the tasks I must complete—laundry, cleaning, the birthday gift I need to buy and mail, phone calls I need to make, people I need to touch base with—after I've rested. Sometimes in order to really rest, I need to get away from the familiar, which means I make a trek somewhere—usually away from home. Once I've worked hard to finally rest, I find my mind and body take a few days to catch up. My brain whirs with all the activity I've left behind, and the adrenaline continues to course through my veins, urging me to keep going.

I find that most of the time when we're all set to rest physically, mentally, spiritually, and emotionally, we're anxious and out of sorts. Any respite from activity makes us feel guilty; the people and situations we leave behind linger on our hearts, and we feel neglectful. The hubbub of life leaves us feeling distant from the Lord and lonely. Sometimes we don't know where to begin once we have time to spend with Him again. And, even if a week's worth of rest or vacation helps, anxiety and troubles bubble to the surface once again upon our return to normal life.

I wonder, do we ever really rest? Do we understand what rest really is?

Jesus said, *"Come to Me, all of you who are weary and carry heavy burdens, and I will give you rest. Take My yoke upon you. Let Me teach you, because I am humble and gentle of heart, and you will find rest for your souls. For My yoke is easy to bear and the burden I give you is light"* (Matthew 11:28-30 NLT). Interesting that Jesus invites us to find rest for our souls—not by the cessation of activity but by coming to Him.

The writer of Hebrews has a lot to say about the believer's rest and how this rest, coupled with faith, is centered in Christ. So, set your cell phone aside, set your computer to "rest," and ask the Lord to free your mind from distraction. Pray He'll speak directly to you as you look into this next section of Hebrews.

DAY ONE

☐ Read Hebrews

Hebrews 3:15-19

Rest: stopping of work or activity, a state or period of refreshing freedom from exertion; freedom from mental or emotional anxiety. (Microsoft Word's Encarta Encyclopedia)

1. What telltale signs in your life remind you that you need physical rest, and do you pay attention? Why or why not?

2. What causes you the most mental, emotional, or spiritual unrest and why?

The writer of Hebrews introduces the subject of true rest at the end of chapter three. It's important to remember the Israelites were slaves in Egypt for 400 years. Every day they faced harsh taskmasters who were never satisfied and always wanted "more bricks" and provided "less straw." So, when Moses came on the scene as Israel's deliverer, you can imagine the jubilation. They were being set free from slavery. That's the initial rest the writer of Hebrews discusses—the rest God promised to the Israelites upon their deliverance from slavery in Egypt. This deliverance is a picture of salvation—God provided rest from physical slavery through a deliverer, Moses. On a grander, more excellent scale, He provides eternal rest from bondage to sin, through the great and perfect Deliverer Jesus Christ.

Remember, the purpose for looking back to this point in Israel's history—Moses and his faithfulness as God's servant; the Israelite's liberation from slavery; the giving of the Ten Commandments; the construction of the Tabernacle and the role of the High Priest—is to show us that each of those events foreshadowed what Jesus Christ eventually fulfilled. This is true regarding the subject of rest, as well.

3. For review, read Hebrews 3:15-19 (NLT). Note that as the writer introduces the subject of rest, he refers back to the Old Testament and in particular Psalm 95:8-11.

    "Remember what it says:
    'Today when you hear his voice,
    don't harden your hearts
    as Israel did when they rebelled.'

    And who was it who rebelled against God, even though they heard his voice? Wasn't it the people Moses led out of Egypt? And who made God angry for forty years? Wasn't it the people who sinned, whose corpses lay in the wilderness? And to whom was God speaking when he took an oath that they would never enter his rest? Wasn't it the people who disobeyed him? So we see that because of their unbelief they were not able to enter his rest."

    Who was unable to enter God's rest and why?

4. I love the Psalms because they soothe, console, and also teach me how to exalt and worship God. Additionally, they provide historical perspective on God's faithfulness in the midst of Israel's wandering and rebellion. Psalm 78 is a great summary of Exodus and Israel's wilderness wanderings.

    a. Read it all the way through in order to grasp the context and look for God's faithfulness and grace.

b. What was the main thing that kept Israel from recognizing God's blessing?

God	**Israel**
Psalm 78:5-7	Psalm 78:8-11
Psalm 78:12-16	Psalm 78:17-20
Psalm 78:24-25, 31	Psalm 78:32
Psalm 78:38	Psalm 78:40-43

c. Describe ways you see and experience God's faithfulness and grace in your life despite your unbelief.

5. a. Read Psalm 81 and record the different things God promised for the children of Israel after freeing them from slavery in Egypt:

Psalm 81:6-7

Psalm 81:10

Psalm 81:14

Psalm 81:16

b. What did God ask of the Israelites?

6. Before we're too hard on Israel, let's step back for a minute. Let's imagine, along with thousands of others, we escaped from Egypt. The Red Sea miraculously parted, and we crossed from slavery to freedom (Sometimes I read that as if it's a normal occurrence.). We now live on the ground in the middle of nowhere. Provisions ran out a few days back, and now we wake and go to sleep listening to the screams of crying babies and hungry kids. Our parched mouths are a relentless reminder there's no water. It would be a constant challenge to trust God, don't you think? What do you learn from Israel's example and God's promises, and how does this help you as you face tough things in your life?

Reflect & Respond

The Lord delivered the Israelites from slavery. He "relieved their shoulder of the burden and freed their hands from the brick load." He demonstrated His power and parted the Red Sea; He protected them from their enemies; He promised abundant blessings—not only external but also internal, spiritual blessings.

I'm amazed at the language in Psalm 81: "Open your mouth wide and I will fill it; I would feed you with the finest of wheat and satisfy you with honey from the rock." He promised, in very rich and full language, He'd provide for their physical and spiritual needs. Yet, they refused to believe Him. As a result, the Israelites wandered in the wilderness for 40 years and never experienced the sweet rest God promised.

In his book, *The Rest of God*, Mark Buchanan writes, *"If only I could get away is our mantra. Then I would be safe. Then I could enjoy my life. But what we find is that flight becomes captivity: once we begin to flee the things that threaten and burden us, there is no end to fleeing."*

"God's solution is surprising. He offers rest. But it's a unique form of rest. It's to rest in him in the midst of our threats and our burdens. It's discovering, as David did in seasons of distress, that God is our rock and refuge right in the thick of our situations." [1]

As I write these words, I can't help but reflect on my own response to my moments or sojourns in my own "wilderness." I'm really no different from the children of Israel. So often when circumstances look bleak, I see no light at the end of the tunnel, and I feel like God has forgotten me. Fear and doubt sneak into my thoughts and heart, and I turn my eyes inward. At this point, it's easy to succumb to my insecurities, to look for temporary solutions to my problems—whether they're looming and large or inconsequential. I'm so thankful for these examples in the Word that remind me to trust Him, to rest in His provision and promises. I love the fact He knows I'm weak and prone to fall apart, which is why I need my Savior every day. I love Jesus' invitation and promise: "Come to Me and I will give you rest," or the words of the psalmist, "When my anxious thoughts multiply within me, Your consolations [comfort or support] delight my soul" (Psalm 94:19 NASB).

@ What do you think it means to rest in the Lord as you walk through your own wilderness?

@ Based on what you've learned about Jesus so far, what truths about Him and His character can you rest in as you walk through your current challenges?

Oh Lord, thank You for inviting me to draw near to You. Thank You for relieving my shoulder of the burdens and brick loads of my life. I cast them on You and gratefully acknowledge that nothing is too difficult for You. Help me to experience the rest that is eternally mine in Christ Jesus and the rest You provide through Him for my daily life.

DAY TWO

☐ Read Hebrews

Hebrews 4:1-7

As I contemplate the subject of rest, I can't help but think about the unbelievers living around me who, because of their unbelief, are perpetually striving for something more and are never able to really stop, rest, or relax. Recently, I listened to a talk on this chapter of Hebrews, and the speaker spoke not only about unbelievers who don't know this place of peaceful and eternal rest in Christ but also about followers of Christ who don't fully enjoy it either. Just like everyone around us, we tend to look for external things to satisfy. We strive and work in order to please God believing our effort will somehow give us a better standing with Him. We're especially proud of ourselves if we spend all of our time "doing" things for God. I wonder, do we ever stop and simply enjoy Him? Are we able to rest in Him in the midst of a full schedule? The speaker exhorted us to "lay down our deadly doing" and enter into the rest of God.

1. Are there moments in your life when you, as God's child, fail to enter into God's rest because you feel you "should" and "ought" to do more in order to make Him happy? If so, describe one of those moments.

2. Read Hebrews 4:1-7 (NLT) and note all the things that keep people from entering God's rest.

"God's promise of entering his rest still stands, so we ought to tremble with fear that some of you might fail to experience it. For this good news—that God has prepared this rest—has been announced to us just as it was to them. But it did them no good because they didn't share the faith of those who listened to God. For only we who believe can enter his rest. As for the others, God said, 'In my anger I took an oath: "They will never enter my place of rest,"' Even though this rest has been ready since he made the world. We know it is ready because of the place in the Scriptures where it mentions the seventh day: 'On the seventh day God rested from all his work.' But in the other passage God said, 'They will never enter my place of rest.'

So God's rest is there for people to enter, but those who first heard this good news failed to enter because they disobeyed God. So God set another time for entering his rest, and that time is today. God announced this through David much later in the words already quoted:

'Today when you hear his voice, don't harden your hearts.'"

Truth Search

3. In his commentary on Hebrews, John MacArthur says:

> *"The basic idea [of rest] is that of ceasing from work or from any kind of action. You stop doing what you are doing....Applied to God's rest, it means no more self-effort as far as salvation is concerned. It means the end of trying to please God by our feeble, fleshly works. God's perfect rest is a rest in free grace.*
>
> *To enter God's rest means to be at peace with God, to possess the perfect peace He gives. It means to be free from guilt and even unnecessary feelings of guilt. It means freedom from worry about sin, because sin is forgiven. God's rest is the end of legalistic works and the experience of peace in the total forgiveness of God."* [2]

a. Look up the following passages and write down what you learn about salvation:
Ephesians 2:8-9

Matthew 11:28-30

Titus 3:4-7

b. What do these passages teach you about "God's place of rest?"

4. I talk with many people who don't believe they're worthy of forgiveness; some don't like the fact that salvation is really "free," and they want to earn it.

a. Based upon what you've learned so far—and from your own experience—why do you think most people have such a hard time entering into God's place of rest through salvation?

b. How would you describe this rest to someone who doesn't know Jesus Christ personally?

5. The idea of rest for a believer is difficult to grasp because life itself isn't restful. How can we really experience this rest if we're diagnosed with breast cancer, or our child is arrested for shoplifting, or school tuition increased beyond our savings, or a family member committed suicide? What does it mean to experience God's rest as described above, and how is it possible?

6. a. Why do you think the writer includes the warning to unbelievers, "Don't harden your hearts"?

b. What might tempt someone to harden her heart toward the Lord and His Gospel?

Reflect & Respond

According to Hebrews 4:7 "God has set another time for entering His rest, and that time is today...." Today when you hear His voice, don't harden your hearts.'" When I read this verse, faces of friends and family who haven't believed in Jesus Christ come to my mind, reminding me to pray that they'll not harden their hearts, but believe. I'm also extremely thankful for the rest that is mine in Christ Jesus, that my salvation is secure in Christ, and that my ongoing relationship with Him is not dependant upon my works. I really can rest in Him and in what He has done for me.

- © Take some time to thank the Lord for the rest that is yours in Christ. Talk with Him about whatever it might be in your life that keeps you from experiencing His rest. Tell him about those areas where unbelief tugs at your heart and tempts you to doubt and lose faith.

- © Write down the names of those for whom you're praying and pray for an opportunity to tell them about the complete rest they can find in Christ. Pray they'll not harden their hearts and will come to faith in Him.

DAY THREE

DIGGING DEEPER

A few years ago I was reading through some of my old journals. As I read, I was struck by how much I was striving. I realized I wasn't really experiencing God's promised rest—the freedom that is mine in Christ. This came at a time when I was studying Galatians—a great epistle on our freedom in Christ. I was challenged to examine my view of God and His grace along with my motives for "doing."

Today we're going to look at some passages that talk about this freedom and rest. If you're struggling to experience God's rich grace and peace, it's my prayer these passages will encourage you. If you're enjoying peaceful rest, then I pray that today's lesson will only add to your worship.

Romans 6-8 is a great section of the New Testament that describes our salvation and freedom in a rich way. We're going to do a quick survey of these three chapters. As you read them, ask the Lord to give you wisdom and insight. Talk to Him about what you need. If you're anxious, ask Him for His peace; if you're distracted, ask Him for focus; if you're doubtful, ask Him for faith.

1. a. Read Romans 6:4, 9-10 and write down what is true of Christ.

    b. Read the following and write down what you learn about all who are "united with Christ."
       Romans 6:2-8

    Romans 6:11, 14

    Romans 6: 16-18

    Romans 6:22-23

2. a. Read Romans 7:14-23. Describe a time recently when you felt like Paul.

    b. Look at Romans 7:24-25. Based upon these verses and Romans 6, why is Jesus Christ the only source of freedom from our battle with the flesh?

    c. Compare this with Romans 6. When you have a "Romans 7" day, what promises in God's Word can you stand on and what truths about you and God can you claim?

3. Romans 8:1 is the pivotal point in these three chapters. Write out the verse and then comment on what it means to you.

4. a. According to Romans 8:5-6 what is the source of peaceful living and why?

b. Describe what this might look like practically in your life.

For Further Study

I remember when I noticed these verses for the first time, and I was astounded. How often I set my mind on the things of the flesh—replaying the day's events or conversations, worrying about events that are several weeks or months out, fretting about what somebody thinks of me, and on and on I go. This verse promises me that when I set my mind on the Spirit—on God—I'll experience life and peace. It's not an automatic, quick fix; but when I choose to talk with the Lord about my problems (however big or small), He soothes my soul. He is the only source of peace—no matter how alluring other solutions may seem.

Jesus said, "In the world you will have tribulation, but be of good cheer, I have overcome the world." Tribulation means, "great difficulty, affliction, or distress." Jesus states with certainty, "You will have tribulation." He also states with authority, "Be of good cheer, I have overcome the world."

The Lord has used the following list of verses to encourage me throughout my life in the face of tribulations. Often I write out these promises to remind me of His faithfulness and the freedom I have to bring my problems to His throne of grace. These are great verses to memorize, as well, because we often need a reminder that Christ is our source of peace and victory.

- John 14:27
- John 16:33
- Philippians 4:6-7
- I Peter 5:6-7
- Psalm 55:22

5. According to the following, what is true of God's Holy Spirit?
    Romans 8:6

Romans 8:13, 15-16

Romans 8:26

6. When I'm anxious about a conversation I need to have, or I'm angry at my husband, or discouraged by my circumstances, I'll "set my mind on the Spirit." I'll try to remember everything that's true of Him. I can talk to Him about my anxiety, I can call on Him to replace my anger with His understanding, or ask Him to lead me through whatever is discouraging me. Sometimes I choose to wait, and I give into my anxiety or lose my temper or wallow in discouragement; but, once I fix my heart and mind on Him, I remember His peace and care. What about you? What helps you remember to set your mind on the Spirit, and how do you choose to be "led by the Spirit"?

7. Finally, look again at Romans 8:1. Now look at Romans 8:35-39. Read it aloud and insert your name: "Who shall separate Cas/me from the love of God...." Thank Him for His never-ending love. Two verses that proclaim two very profound and transforming truths: Romans 8:1 (no condemnation) and Romans 8:39 (no separation, all because of Jesus Christ).

    Sometimes when I feel anxious or worried, unworthy or unlovable, I'll write down all that I'm thinking and feeling, and then I'll write Romans 8:1 and 35-39 over the top. It's one way of "setting my mind on the Spirit and experiencing life and peace."

    Write down your anxieties and worries, your insecurities and feelings of unworthiness—whatever distracts you from believing what's true of you because of Christ. Lay those at the feet of Jesus, and call on His Spirit to help you hear and respond to the truth. Ask Him to lead you and then write Romans 8:1 and 8:35-39 over the top. Thank Him for His love and grace lavished on you at the cross.

Reflect & Respond

What helps make Jesus and the Bible and following Him more real for me is choosing to bring Him into thought processes and situations that could so easily consume all of my energy.

- Time and again, the issues that cost me the most emotional energy are those that cause me to question my value and standing before God. And, while it may be overly dramatic to think a decision would separate me from the love of God, I can feel that way nonetheless. Frequently, in the midst of hard things, I'll be cognizant of God's presence as I fret and stew, but it's not until I finally sit down and have a conversation with Him that I find the rest and peace He promises. When I go back over passages like Romans 6, I'm reminded in that very moment He's present, powerful, and my source of life and peace. It's not about me; it's about Him.

- Most of us live at a frenetic pace. There's always more to do and less time. I like what Mark Buchanan says about liberty and rest: *"At the heart of liberty—of being let go—is worship. But at the heart of worship is rest—a stopping from all work, all worry, all scheming, all fleeing—to stand amazed and thankful before God and his work. There can be no real worship without true rest."* [3]

Are you able to take time to worship, to stand and thank Him for His work in and around you? This week try to stop and rest in Him. Enjoy His creation and His creativity. Take a walk around the block and watch for His creativity. Go on a drive into the country where it's quiet. Meander the city blocks and see His image in the faces of those who pass you by. Wherever you are, take a deep breath and rest in Him.

Worship Him for liberating you from the power of sin. Stand amazed. Thank God for His work on your behalf.

DAY FOUR

☐ Read Hebrews

Hebrews 4:8-13

Tom Wright, in his commentary entitled *Hebrews for Everyone*, writes, *"We are faced, then, with a sequence of three 'rests'; God's own rest on the seventh day of creation; the 'rest' which Joshua gave the people when he brought them into the promised land; and the future 'rest' which the Psalm [95] promised, and which, according to Hebrews, remains still as a promise looking into the future."* [4]

The Israelites wandered for 40 long years in the desert and suffered the consequence of unbelief and faithlessness. God, however, was faithful and used Joshua to lead a new generation into the Promised Land and the promised rest. The rest Joshua provided is a historical picture of deliverance from slavery (Deuteronomy 5:12-15). But, as our passage indicates, this rest wasn't lasting, because it was a physical rest. The real final rest, which is still to come, is possible all because of Jesus Christ.

As we look ahead to that final rest and at the role of God's Word in our lives, take time to pray for a soft and teachable heart.

1. a. Read Hebrews 4:8-11 (NLT) once again: *Now if Joshua had succeeded in giving them this rest, God would not have spoken about another day of rest still to come. So there is a special rest still waiting for the people of God. For all who have entered into God's rest have rested from their labors, just as God did after creating the world. So let us do our best to enter that rest. But if we disobey God, as the people of Israel did, we will fall.*

   b. Read the following and write down what you learn about the future rest (We'll look at this more in-depth in future lessons.).
   Hebrews 11:10

   Hebrews 11:13-16

Hebrews 12:22-24

Wright says, *"Some Christians today live in long-established churches where everything is in danger of getting a bit sleepy; nobody can really believe it can be as good as it was in the old days (which are usually, of course, a romantic fiction). Other Christians live in churches which are struggling for survival within a hostile environment.…All of us face the challenge to trust God rather than to trust the way we feel or the things we see in front of us. All of us need to keep before our eyes the promise of God's eventual, and eternal 'rest'…. If it's relaxation you want, don't expect too much of it in the present Christian life; but remember that you are promised a real 'rest' at the end! The road to 'rest' is labeled 'belief', 'holding on', 'keeping a firm grip on the confession of faith'."* [5]

2. How do you keep the promise of God's eventual and eternal rest before your eyes, and why do you think it takes "belief and a firm grip"?

3. a. Interestingly, this whole passage on rest is followed by Hebrews 4:12-13 (NLT). What is true of God's Word according to these two verses? *"For the word of God is alive and powerful. It is sharper than the sharpest two-edged sword, cutting between soul and spirit, between joint and marrow. It exposes our innermost thoughts and desires. Nothing in all creation is hidden from God. Everything is naked and exposed before his eyes, and he is the one to whom we are accountable."*

    b. Based upon what you've gathered and learned from this passage so far about belief, obedience, and rest, why do you think the writer switches our attention to God, His Word, and our nakedness?

4. a. Why do you think having our innermost thoughts and desires exposed by God's Word can aid us in our belief and in our rest?

    b. What do you think it means to be held accountable by God and His Word?

Reflect & Respond

There are seasons in my life when my time in the Word wanes. I get busy and choose not to rest at the feet of Jesus. Oh, I grab some snippets here and there, but I miss out on the real nourishment that only the Word offers. I find during these "lean" times I quickly lose perspective. I become prideful, cowardly, or simply lukewarm. I look at what's around me rather than what's ahead. Ultimately, we all tend to look inward rather than upward to Jesus. But, when we open up the Word, the Spirit reminds us we can pour out our troubles to Him. If we're struggling with our attitude or unbelief, the Spirit uses His sword to convict us and to remind us that Jesus Christ gave His life as a sacrifice for our sin. There's something terrible (He knows everything about us.) and comforting (He loves us and wants us to draw near.) about being "open and laid bare" before our Great High Priest and His Word. Each time we experience the surgical skill of God's Word on our attitude, unbelief, or doubts, we're drawn closer. We'll find ourselves longing for more of Him and less of "me."

As we allow the Spirit to do His work through the Word, it helps to remember, "The written word is all about the Living Word. Words on pages point to the great self-giving God in the Word made flesh.... Words ever so fragile, words so easily disregarded or dismissed, are the way God chooses to engage us. And in case we are inclined to think that mere words amount to little, God has embodied that word in Jesus Christ. Christ becomes the visible and substantial Word. A Word that spells deed. A Word that is active. A Word that can make one whole!

Indeed! This is no mere Word. It is a life-giving and life-transforming Word. A Word that lives in us through the Spirit, reorienting us to new ways of being. Ways that have to do with forgiveness, peace-making, reconciliation and healing.

In the mystery of faith a Word can open up a new world. In the brooding presence of the Spirit a Word can transform us. In the power of the Word made flesh a Word can heal us." [6]

@ Describe a time when you experienced the work of God's Word in a penetrating way in your life.

Ah, the Word of God is living and active and became flesh, Jesus Christ. Wow, what a Savior!

DAY FIVE

If you're like me, rest is something you look forward to, sometimes from the moment you get up in the morning! Our fast-paced lives seem to rarely slow down—ongoing activity, jobs that are never complete, to-do lists that have no end, ladders we try to climb, ambition that is never satisfied, and contentment that is unrealized. I've often wondered, is this really how God wants us to live? Is my satisfaction in Him, and do I believe He's fully satisfied with me because of Christ?

When restlessness surfaces in your life, pay attention. When worry surfaces to the point of all out anxiety, when you find yourself striving yet never experiencing deep satisfaction, when you realize that it's impossible for you to stop, really stop, striving—pay attention.

1. Ask yourself, "What is keeping me from experiencing the deep rest that God promises?" If you know Christ as your Savior, the rest is already yours, because Jesus delivered you from slavery to sin (Romans 6). Enjoy that blessed place, enjoy your blessed Savior who did the work for you, and rest in Him. Review this amazing truth once again by looking at the following passages:

    Romans 5:1

    Romans 6:3

    Romans 8:14

2. This rest is for anyone who believes that Jesus is Lord. If you've yet to place your faith in Christ, you'll never know the peace that comes through Him. Let me encourage you to surrender your life to the only One who can give you rest from guilt and sin. Come to Jesus and He will give you rest.

3. As I spent time in this chapter of Hebrews, I was challenged on all sides regarding the believer's rest. In particular, the Lord began to press me to think more seriously about the Sabbath. We read in Hebrews 4:4 that God rested on the seventh day from all His works, and the Fourth Commandment says to "remember the Sabbath day and keep it holy." Physical rest is important to God. Jesus' words in Mark 2:27, "The Sabbath was made for man, and not man for the Sabbath" challenged me, too. God set aside a day for me to stop everything else and enjoy Him.

"Sabbath is a foretaste and a heralding of eternity. Its joy is precisely this: it rehearses heaven" (Abraham Joshua Heschel).

4. So, over the past several months, I've begun to think of the Sabbath as a way to "imitate God's divine example" and enjoy Him and His creation. Honestly, it hasn't been easy. As I try to rest and enjoy the day, I find myself counting the hours until the sun sets so I can get back to "doing." It's not easy to rest, but it's freeing when I do.

5. Are you taking the time you need at the Lord's throne of grace? How might you benefit from a day of "rest" in light of all that we've discovered this week? Reflect back over the last four days and review what we've studied. Contemplate what you've learned about your freedom and liberty in Christ. Maybe, like me, you need to "herald eternity and rehearse heaven" more often by resting. Talk to the Lord about what real, Sabbath rest looks like for you.

For Further Study

Another of God's attributes is His immutability. Nothing about God or His purpose ever changes.

I love the fact that we can depend upon God to never change. His love, grace, and mercy never change nor do His righteousness or holiness.

- Look at the following verses and passages.
  Psalm 102-25-27

  Malachi 3:6-7

  Hebrews 13:8

- As you consider your own life along with the world in general, what does it mean to you personally to know God never changes?

---

1 Mark Buchanan, *The Rest of God* (Nashville: W Publishing Group, 2006), p.17.

2 John MacArthur, *The MacArthur Bible Commentary Hebrews* (Chicago: Moody Bible Institute, 1983), pp. 98-99.

3 Buchanan, p. 94.

4 N.T. Wright. *Hebrews for Everyone* (Perthshire: Ashford Colour Press, 2004), 41

5 Ibid

6 Charles Ringma, *The Seeking Heart* (Brewster: Paraclete Press, 2006), p. 64.

Jesus, Our Wonderful Counselor

Hebrews 4:14-5:6; 7-10

"God…has spoken to us in His Son, whom He appointed heir of all things, through whom also He made the world. And He is the radiance of His glory and the exact representation of His nature, and upholds all things by the word of His power. When He had made purification of sins, He sat down at the right hand of the Majesty on high…" (Hebrews 1:1-3). He was the perfect sacrifice, His blood was pure and holy, and His death satisfied the wrath of God.

We've learned that because He is fully God and fully man—perfect in every way—He delivers us from sin and death; He sanctifies and sets us free from slavery to sin, and because of His willing sacrifice, we can rest.

We've looked at the power of God's word—a two-edged sword that pierces and judges the thoughts and intentions of our hearts. We've discovered the extent of God's presence—no creature is hidden from His sight, "all things are open and laid bare to the eyes of Him with whom we have to do." All the gook and grime in our hearts is exposed, open, and laid bare. The strong, powerful, revealing Word of God is followed by the Great High Priest and His throne of grace to which we may run whenever we need mercy to help. Although you and I are naked before Him, He has provided His Son, our Savior, to show us love, mercy, grace, and forgiveness—not because of anything we do but because of who He is and what He has done. It is at the foot of His throne we find true rest—His gift of grace.

In this lesson we'll discover why Jesus, the Great High Priest, is no comparison to the Old Testament priesthood, and why the new covenant is superior to the old. We'll meet Melchizedek, a mysterious king and priest first introduced to Abraham, and we'll also reflect upon the fact that we're free to draw near with confidence to God's throne of grace.

DAY ONE

☐ Read Hebrews

Hebrews 4:14-5:6

Remember, Hebrews is written to Jewish believers who knew all about Moses, the Ten Commandments, priests, and the tabernacle. The writer takes great care to show how each of these were merely a shadow or copy of what was to come in Jesus Christ.

The next several chapters show how He is superior to the Old Testament priesthood, how the new covenant is better than the old, and how Christ's sacrifice is superior and final. In this lesson, we'll look at Hebrews 4:14-5:10 and 7:1-8:13 and focus on Christ as the superior High Priest and what this means for us as His children and His ambassadors.

Proverbs 2:6-7 says, *"For the LORD gives wisdom; from His mouth come knowledge and understanding. He stores up sound wisdom for the upright; He is a shield to those who walk in integrity."* I love the fact that He gives us wisdom and stores up sound wisdom for us. Pray that He will give you understanding as you dive into these great chapters of Hebrews. There's no doubt that this is a complicated book of Scripture, and we'll need His wisdom to walk us through.

1. We're going to begin by doing an overview of what the next few chapters have to say about the role of the high priest and compare the high priest of the Old Testament with the great High Priest—Jesus the Son of God. Before we look at Hebrews, I've chosen various chapters and passages that will help refresh your memory on the role of the priests and the rituals they performed. As you read, keep Jesus in mind—our great High Priest.

   a. Read the following and record what you learn about the Old Testament priesthood. Remember that Aaron (the brother of Moses) was the first high priest:
   Exodus 28:1

   Numbers 8:24-25

   Leviticus 10:8-11

Numbers 18:21-24

b. Read the following and record the various duties of the Old Testament priest:
Exodus 30:7-10

Leviticus 8:8-21

Numbers 18:21, 26

Deuteronomy 17:8-13

Notice that no matter how "elevated" the priesthood was, no matter how beautiful the garments, no matter how holy their position, they were flawed, imperfect, and sinful just like you and me. Only Jesus Christ is the perfect High Priest.

2. Now read Hebrews 5:1-4 and answer the following questions:

a. From whom was every high priest in the Old Testament selected and for what purpose (Hebrews 5:1, 4)?

b. According to Hebrews 5:2-3 what qualifies him as high priest and what's he obligated to do?

3.   Remember, God has spoken to us in His Son. Record what you learn about Jesus as our great
     High Priest:
     Hebrews 4:15

     Hebrews 5:5-6, 10 (Who appointed Christ as High Priest?)

     Hebrews 5:7-8

     Hebrews 5:9

The vast contrast between priests "taken from among men" and Jesus, the high priest designated by God, is obvious. In many ways, those taken among men embody for us the weakness and frailty of human beings. No matter how hard a Levitical priest tried, he was never perfect. He offered sacrifices for his sin as well as everyone else's. Aaron's sons, among the first to hold the office of priest, disobeyed God's instructions almost immediately and were put to death; the rest of Jewish history reveals corrupt and rebellious men holding the office as priest. However, Jesus, our High Priest, is a picture of the glory and majesty of God—perfect in every way. His offering is also a picture of His amazing grace. Never, under any circumstances, could anyone obtain this standard of perfection.

4.   Based upon what you've learned so far, what does Christ's role as High Priest mean for us, his
     children (keep your eyes on Hebrews 4:14-16)?

Reflection

We can draw near to the throne of grace with confidence...I love that. However, I don't think I grasp the full implication of this privilege until I reflect back on the Old Testament—and even then I don't think I fully grasp the significance. The pages of Leviticus paint a very weighty and bloody picture. The graphic ritual of sacrifice detailed throughout the pages of Leviticus reminds us sin was/is serious and forgiveness demanded a price—a price that was paid over and over again.

God, though ever present, seemed very distant and ominous. Only a select few were allowed into His presence and took great care before they stepped into His presence.

"[Jesus Christ] became the final Priest and the final Sacrifice. Sinless, he did not offer sacrifices for himself. Immortal, he never has to be replaced. Human, he could bear human sins. Therefore he did not offer sacrifices for himself; he offered himself as the final sacrifice. There will never be the need for another. There is one mediator between us and God. One priest. We need no other. Oh, how happy are those who draw near to God through Christ alone." [1]

DAY TWO

☐ Read Hebrews

Hebrews 7:23-28

We're going to dive into Hebrews 7 and 8 to see what more we can learn about our High Priest. Once again, pray for God's wisdom. He is the source of understanding. Pray for the ability to listen to and hear from the Spirit as you study these great truths.

1. Review Day One. Refresh your memory on the difference between the priests taken from among men and Jesus Christ, appointed by God.

2. Read Hebrews 7:23-28. Record what you learn about the former priests and what you learn about Jesus:

	Jesus	**Priests**
Hebrews 7:23		
Hebrews 7:24		
Hebrews 7:25		
Hebrews 7:26-27		
Hebrews 7:28		

We've learned so far that every high priest taken from among men was appointed on behalf of men; he, according to the old covenant, was taken from the tribe of Levi. He had to offer sacrifice for the sins of the people and for his own sin, daily, because he was a weak sinner just like everybody else. We learned that these priests existed in greater numbers because they were temporal. Someone needed to take their place when they died.

On the other hand, God appointed Jesus. He wasn't from the tribe of Levi like Aaron, but He was from the tribe of Judah. "For it was evident that our Lord was descended from Judah, a tribe with reference to which Moses spoke nothing concerning priests" (Hebrews 8:14). Because of this we're going to learn "when the priesthood is changed, of necessity there takes place a change of law also" (Hebrews 7:15).

Jesus is different, set apart. He doesn't have daily needs, and though tempted in all things, He never sinned. He is eternal and holds His position as priest forever/permanently and is able to save forever those who draw near to God.

Quoting from the prophecy of Psalm 110, the writer of Hebrews tells us Jesus became a high priest according to the order of Melchizedek (Hebrews 5:6, 6:20, and 7:15). So, we now learn that there isn't just the Levitical priesthood, but there's a new and completely different Priesthood.

3. a. Look at Hebrews 7:1-3 and record what you learn about Melchizedek that is true of Jesus, as well (keep your eyes on the text).

    b. Read Hebrews 7:4-11. How was the people's encounter with a Levitical priest similar to Abraham's encounter with Melchizedek, and why is it significant that Abraham was blessed by Melchizedek?

4. Hebrews 7:18-24 gives us a series of contrasts between the former commandment (the Law), the former priesthood, and the better hope and better priest—Jesus. List those contrasts:

Former Commandment	Former Priest	Jesus
7:18 Set aside, weak, useless		
7:19 Made nothing perfect		
7:21		
7:22		

7:23

7:24

7:25

Everything in this passage leads up to the fact that Jesus is able to save forever those who draw near to God through Him. Let that ring in your soul for a minute. He lives to make intercession for you and me and every believer through the ages. He is our Priest and our Advocate, and He stands in the presence of God on our behalf. Nothing can ever change our standing before God because of Jesus Christ.

Reflection

We've covered a lot of ground today—ground that Bible students throughout the ages have wrestled with. What's most important is: "We have a high priest, who has taken His seat at the right hand of the throne of the Majesty in the heavens" (Hebrews 8:1).

"Some Christians face the danger of forgetting just how central and vital Jesus himself was and is to ever aspect of Christian faith. It is possible to get so wrapped up in theological technicalities or practical details that Jesus comes into the equation, if at all, almost as an afterthought. Hebrews ought to provide a strong antidote to any such tendencies. This writer can't get enough of thinking through who Jesus was and is and what he achieved in his death and in the new life that emerged on the other side. That alone is worth a good deal of pondering." [2]

@ Ponder Jesus before you close your Bible and go on with your day.

He is eternal and indestructible

He is able to save forever those who come to Him

He is my Advocate

He is holy and innocent

He is perfectly sinless and exalted above the heavens forever

He is separate from sinners and yet calls us to draw near

He offered up Himself because of His grace and mercy

@ As you look ahead to your day or week, what about Jesus encourages you as you face the day or gives you energy to press forward and why?

If you're like me, then sometimes it's hard to bring Jesus into the here and now. He can feel distant or uninvolved in the daily stuff of life. We forget to pray or ask for help; and sometimes we're just plain tired. For the past few days I've felt a little like this. Reading this chapter has encouraged me. Jesus is my Great High Priest, and I can draw near to His throne to find help for every need—inconsequential or gigantic. He's always right here.

DAY THREE

☐ Read Hebrews

Excerpts from Hebrews 8, 9, 10

Typically Day Three is reserved for more focused study, but in this lesson, I'd like to reserve that for Day Four. We've looked at the superiority of Christ as our great High Priest, and how the Old Testament priesthood was "a copy and a shadow of the heavenly things" that would be fulfilled in Christ. In a similar way, the Old Testament covenant, or law, was put in place as a "tutor to lead us to Christ, that we may be justified (declared righteous) by faith" (Galatians 3:24 NASB). Today we're going to look at how the new covenant, in Christ, is superior to the old covenant.

Remember that the overarching theme of Hebrews is the superiority of Jesus Christ. One of my prayers is that we'd walk away from our study of Hebrews with a greater desire to worship Jesus, because we have a deeper, richer understanding of who He is and the purpose for which He had to offer Himself as a sacrifice for our sin.

Today we're going to look at the purpose of the Old Covenant and why the New Covenant in Christ is superior. Remember that the Law or Covenant is the bond that was established between God and Israel at Mount Sinai. By setting forth the superiority of the New Covenant in Christ, the Hebrew writer isn't saying that the Old Covenant was bad but explains its purpose and fulfillment.

Pray that your heart and mind will receive what the Lord has for you today. Ask Him to help you see not only the truth of these passages but also comprehend what it all means for you today.

1. Read the following passages and record what you learn about the Law:
   Hebrews 7:18-19; 8:7-9

   Hebrews 9:16-22

   Hebrews 10:1-8

2. Compare the Hebrews passages with the following and write any additional insight you gain regarding the Law:

    Galatians 2:16

    Galatians 3:10-11

    Galatians 3:24

3. Jesus Christ ushers in a brand-new covenant, and because He is the great High Priest, He is the mediator of a better covenant. Read the following and write what you learn about Jesus and this "better" covenant:

    Hebrews 8:6, 9-13

    Hebrews 9:11-15

    Hebrews 9:23-28

    Hebrews 10:10-18

4. Read and record II Corinthians 3:5-6. What insight do you gain from this verse regarding the new covenant?

"The suffering and death of Christ guarantees the inner change of his people (the law written on their hearts) and the forgiveness of their sins.

To guarantee that this covenant will not fail, Christ takes the initiative to create the faith and secure the faithfulness of his people. He brings a new-covenant people into being by writing the law not just on stone, but on the heart…This is the spiritual life that enables us to see and believe the glory of Christ. This miracle creates the new-covenant people. It is sure and certain because Christ bought it with His own blood." [3]

> 5. Continue reading II Corinthians 3:7-11 and record what more you learn about the old covenant (the bond between God and Israel made at Mount Sinai in the Old Testament) and then what you learn about the New Covenant that is fulfilled in Christ.

Reflection

"Now the Lord is the Spirit; and where the Spirit of the Lord is, there is liberty. But we all, with unveiled face beholding as in a mirror the glory of the Lord, are being transformed into the same image from glory to glory, just as from the Lord, the Spirit" (II Corinthians 3:17-18). Reflect on the truth of these two verses— we are being transformed by the Spirit of the Lord.

> ⓔ It is remarkable and humbling to realize that we both behold and display the glory of the Lord because of His Spirit who lives in us and because Jesus Christ has made us adequate as servants of a new covenant. In what ways have you seen and experienced the transforming work of the Spirit in your life recently?

> ⓔ From your experience, how do you know the Spirit of the Lord brings liberty and freedom?

Ⓒ Maybe you're living in bondage to a habit or a sin that you know isn't pleasing to the Lord; maybe you're unsure of God's unfailing and unconditional love; perhaps you've fallen back into your old way of life. Based upon what you've discovered, how can you enjoy the liberating freedom that only Christ offers?

DAY FOUR

☐ Read Hebrews

Digging Deeper

We've spent a lot of time surveying the Levitical priesthood, touching on the divine regulations that God set in place for worship, and considering the incredible detail and precision required to fulfill the laws of worship. As I read through the pages of Leviticus, I'm struck every time by the number of regulations and the bloodiness of the worship. I wonder, how did the priests remember all of those details? I also wonder what went through the minds of the Israelites. Obviously, they were not free to draw near to the throne of grace, and I doubt that anyone felt "confident" in this endeavor.

I don't want to take for granted that because of Jesus Christ I can draw near, confidently, all day long to God's throne of grace. The veil that separated me and you from the Holy One was ripped in two when Jesus died—He paved the way to the Father's throne. Today we're going to ponder this great truth for ourselves.

Biblical commentator and pastor John Piper writes, *"We are likely to feel unwelcome in the presence of God if we come with struggles. We feel God's purity and perfection so keenly that everything about us seems unsuitable in his presence. But then we remember that Jesus is 'sympathetic.' He feels with us, not against us. This awareness of Christ's sympathy makes us bold to come. He knows our cry. He tasted our struggle. He bids us come with confidence when we feel our need."* [4]

Hannah, a young woman in the Old Testament, provides an excellent picture of someone who drew near to the throne of grace and found mercy to help in her time of need. What is interesting about her story is that it takes place under the Law. But I think it points forward to the reality of what we can experience now under the new covenant because of Jesus.

1. a. Read I Samuel 1:1-8 and summarize Hannah's situation (include not only her circumstances but also her emotions).

   b. What fact is included which indicates she lived under the Old Testament?

2. Continue reading I Samuel 1:9-18. What do you learn about her emotional state from this section of the story, and how does that affect her prayer to the Lord?

3. How would you describe Eli's response to Hannah, and how would you feel if you were in her shoes at this point?

4. In I Samuel 1:15, Hannah explains to Eli she has "poured out her soul" to the Lord.

    a. What do you learn about her faith and depth of relationship with Him?

    b. First Samuel 1:19 tells us that Hannah worshipped before the Lord before she returned home to Ramah. What does this response tell you about her faith in God?

5. a. Read I Samuel 1:20-28 and summarize what takes place over the next three-plus years. What more do you learn from Hannah and her relationship with the Lord from this part of the story (Keep in mind she is an Israelite and lives under the Law.)?

    b. Take a peek at I Samuel 2:21 and record how the Lord continued to bless Hannah even after she left Samuel at the temple.

    c. Is there any indication that Hannah did anything to deserve God's grace and mercy or the blessing of a child? Why is this significant?

6. First Samuel 2:1-10 is "Hannah's Psalm." It's a song of praise and thanks to God who provided for her a child in her distress. Read it aloud and then record the truths about Him that stand out to you and those that speak to you in your current circumstances or emotional state of mind. Worship Him, enjoy His unchanging character, and praise Him for Jesus, the perfect High Priest who makes it possible for us to draw near to the throne of amazing grace.

Reflect & Respond

Hannah, from what we can tell, poured out her soul before the Lord at the doorpost of the temple. I love this picture not only of Hannah but also of God. He is always available to hear and listen to prayers of faith. "He is near to the brokenhearted and saves those who are crushed in spirit" (Psalm 34:18 NASB). Hannah is a great example of a woman who loved God and sought Him for comfort. In Christ Jesus we can freely draw near (anytime day or night), with bold confidence, to the throne once hidden behind a veil and into the very presence of the living God. We can lay it all down at His feet—no matter how huge or trivial our needs are He is there to sympathize, to extend His grace and mercy to help us. It is there we can finally rest.

© In what ways do you identify with Hannah—either in her struggle, her victory, her faith in God?

© What do you take away from her example?

DAY FIVE

☐ Read Hebrews

1. What circumstances or feelings cause you to question whether God is "for" you or "against" you?

2. What inadequacy, bad habit, or ongoing sin ("I shouldn't be struggling with this anymore. I've been a Christian too long.") keeps you from drawing near to His throne? What truth have you found about Jesus in Hebrews that encourages you to press close to Him?

3. Describe a recent experience in which you encountered mercy to help in time of need. Linger here for a moment. If there's something that has held you back from sitting at the feet of Jesus—anything—talk to Him about it. If it's sin, confess it, and then thank Him for washing you with the blood of His sacrifice. Thank Him that you've been purified. If you're burdened by something you consider trivial, talk to Him. Nothing is too big or small for Jesus. Take comfort in the fact that relying on Him is better than relying on our good works or a system of rules and regulations.

For Further Study

God is omniscient and omnipresent, which means that He is always and everywhere present and knows everything. This is terrifying and comforting. As a young believer, I listened to some messages on the attributes of God, and I remember being amazed by the fact that God is always present everywhere. I couldn't hide from Him or choose things I wanted Him to see. He saw (and sees) it all. He also knows everything about you and me. He has no limitations like we do—that's why we can seek Him for the wisdom we lack and trust Him with things we don't understand.

- Read the following passages and write down your observations about God's omnipresence and omniscience:
    Psalm 139:6-11

    Jeremiah 23:23-24

    Job 34:21

    Psalm 33:13-18

- How does God's omnipresence and omniscience encourage you today in your walk with Him?

1 John Piper, *The Passion of Jesus Christ* (Wheaton: Crossways, 2004), p. 71.

2 Tom Wright, *Hebrews for Everyone.* (Perthshire: Ashford Colour Press, 2004). p. 80.

3 Tom Wright, *Hebrews for Everyone* (Perthshire: Ashford Colour Press, 2004) p. 47

4 John Piper, *The Passion of Jesus Christ* (Wheaton: Crossways, 2004), p. 73

Press On to Maturity

Hebrews 5:11-6:20

Hebrews 6 contains challenging, and sometimes confusing, truth. So, for several weeks, I've prayed for wisdom as I begin to write this week's lesson. Yesterday I received this e-mail from a dear friend (she wishes to remain anonymous), who the Lord used to remind me what Hebrews is all about and why we're tackling this complex book.

"Wouldn't it be wonderful to see Jesus again through the eyes of a child, as a new believer does—fully trusting, excited, and amazed at The Truth that set us free? I'll always hope to be as joyful as when I first believed. Let me never get old and crusty, proud and stale, in my knowledge of Him. May I resist when Satan tempts me to go back to my old way of rituals and routines, instead of to the new way that set me free. And I pray I conduct myself in such a way that it encourages others in their walk with Jesus."

I wonder, did the Hebrew believers lose sight of "the truth that set them free"? The writer of Hebrews is obviously concerned about their perspective throughout the book. He warns them to pay attention—don't drift away, beware of evil and hardened hearts that lead to unbelief, and ultimately, take your great salvation and Savior seriously.

It's helpful to remember, and seems apparent from the context, that among those who received this letter were some who had yet to place their faith in Christ. They were involved with believers and seemed to participate in things of the Lord, but they "neglected" salvation and were warned against being "hardened by the deceitfulness of sin." The root of this neglect and hardness is, and always has been, unbelief—taking the attention off of Jesus Christ and putting it on self or circumstances. Hebrews 6 contains a warning for those who have become "dull of hearing" and have "tasted the good things to come, but have fallen away." It's always tempting for true believers to fear "falling away." Let's remember Jesus is able to "save forever those who draw near to Him." When the temptation to question your salvation's security arises, look to Jesus and the cross. He secures your salvation. We'll discuss this topic more in coming lessons.

As I've read and meditated on this chapter, it has helped me to "consider Jesus." The writer clearly wants to exalt Him above all else, to keep Him at the center and as the focus. He begins with stern warnings, then emphasizes the unconditional promise of God, and ends with a sure and steadfast hope—Jesus, the anchor of our soul.

As you begin the lesson today, pray the Lord will soften your heart to receive His truth. Thank Him that His Holy Spirit, who is your teacher (John 14:26), lives in you—you're His home. He is all wise and faithful. Enjoy your time with Him today.

DAY ONE

☐ Read Hebrews

Hebrews 5:11-6:8

As we move into this passage of Hebrews, it feels as though the writer sidetracks from his focus on Jesus as the superior High Priest and pauses to offer a stern warning. As I mentioned earlier, I think it's because there was unbelief in their midst—men and women who were in danger of "repeating the unbelief of the Israelites in the wilderness and failing, therefore, to enter into the spiritual rest which they had been promised." In essence, they weren't taking Christ seriously.

With each warning in this chapter, we tend to feel a tension of sorts. On the one hand, Christ made purification for the sins of undeserving, rebellious people like you and me, and He comes to the aid of those who are tempted and gives mercy to help in time of need. It's essential as Christians we understand that we are justified (declared righteous) in Christ. God loves us with a deep and incomprehensible love (Ephesians 3:16-18). Because of His amazing love He sent Christ to die for our sins. We did nothing to deserve or earn our salvation. We do nothing to keep our salvation—it's secure in Christ. It's vital we remember He is God. His work on the cross is underscored by the fact that He is the Creator and Sustainer of all things. He is holy and just and worthy of our obedience.

I'm not sure why, but sometimes it's easy to take a ho-hum approach to our faith. Life crowds in, and at times, we can take Him and our salvation for granted—we're glad to know our sins are forgiven and that we're going to heaven. But, there's so much more to this relationship. So much more to learn and know about Him.

As you crack open Hebrews today, thank Him for His Spirit who lives in you and gives you the ability to understand these truths; thank Him for His power that enables you to live for Him. Pray that this chapter will stimulate and sharpen your desire to follow Jesus.

1. Read Hebrews 5:11-6:8 in The New Living Translation:

    There is much more we would like to say about this, but it is difficult to explain, especially since you are spiritually dull and don't seem to listen. You have been believers so long now that you ought to be teaching others. Instead, you need someone to teach you again the basic things about God's word—You are like babies who need milk and cannot eat solid food. For someone who lives on milk is still an infant and doesn't know how to do what is right. Solid food is for those who are mature, who through training have the skill to recognize the difference between right and wrong.

    So let us stop going over the basic teachings about Christ again and again. Let us go on instead and become mature in our understanding. Surely we don't need to start again with the fundamental importance of repenting from evil deeds and placing our faith in God. You don't need further instruction about baptisms, the laying on of hands, the resurrection of the dead, and eternal judgment. And so, God willing, we will move forward to further understanding.

For it is impossible to bring back to repentance those who were once enlightened—those who have experienced the good things of heaven and shared in the Holy Spirit, who have tasted the goodness of the word of God and the power of the age to come—and who then turn away from God. It is impossible to bring such people back to repentance; by rejecting the Son of God, they themselves are nailing him to the cross once again and holding him up to public shame.

When the ground soaks up the falling rain and bears a good crop for the farmer, it has God's blessing. But if a field bears thorns and thistles, it is useless. The farmer will soon condemn that field and burn it.

2. Reflect back to Hebrews 5:7-10. Jesus is described as a Son, obedient and perfect, and the source of eternal salvation, and designated by God as a high priest according to the order of Melchizedek. Hebrews 5:11 indicates the writer wanted to say much more about our great High Priest and the order of Melchizedek, but their spiritual dullness kept him from explaining this further.

a. What do you think it means to be "dull of hearing?"

b. What might cause this dullness?

3. According to Hebrews 5:11-13, what is the cause of their immaturity, and what should be true of them by this point?

In his commentary on Hebrews, Ray Stedman writes, "*If they had been growing as they should, they ought by now to be able to pass the great truths of the faith along to others. They would no longer be learning elementary truths of God's word for themselves but could be teachers of those coming after them. The high priestly ministry which Jesus wants them to learn represents an advance on the introductory truths of the Christian faith. But instead of responding to his exhortations they seem to require those basic truths to be explained to them again. At best, they are spiritual infants who need to be taught over and over the elementary truths as a baby needs to be fed milk and is not ready for solid food. At worst, they are not Christians at all, but are like many of the Israelites in the wilderness. They also are in danger of failing to act in faith on the teaching they have received.*"[1]

4. a. Look closely at Hebrews 6:1-2. What are the dull of hearing exhorted to do and why?

b. Why do you think it's beneficial to move beyond the fundamental teachings mentioned here?

Taken in the context of what we've read and studied so far, a vital aspect of true rest (Hebrews 4) is grasping the depth of "the word of righteousness." Once we have received Christ as our Lord and Savior, we are declared righteous. We don't work for or earn our salvation. God is pleased with and loves us absolutely and completely because we're in Christ. It's because of His unchanging love that we're free to rest completely in Him. His Spirit lives in us. Therefore, as we walk with Him, spend time in His Word, and listen, the Spirit trains us to discern good from evil and empowers us to lay aside evil deeds. Because of what Christ has done in and through us, we're transformed and supernaturally able to teach others about our Savior Jesus. As we grow from being a "babe" in Christ and mature, we're able to comprehend the deeper things of the Spirit and grasp the fundamental truths of the gospel in a more profound way.

5. From these verses it seems as though the outward appearance of spirituality distracted them from what was freely given to them in Christ Jesus.

   a. What activities are you involved in that are purely "good works"—that is, activities that you consider the "right" things to do because they make you feel better about yourself, or you think they make God feel better about you?

   b. How can you take what you've learned about Jesus in Hebrews and deepen your experience of taking communion, participating in worship or prayer, evangelism, or reading your Bible?

Reflect & Respond

My life and ministry experience tell me we're all prone to becoming spiritually dull and consequently falling into a religious rut. We go through the motions of being a Christian and sort of "sideline" Jesus. We don't forget about Him, but for a variety of reasons we allow Him and all that He represents to become a bit hazy. That's why the writer exhorts us to "press on to maturity." And, that's why I love Hebrews: it points us to this awesome One who is God.

My friend Dorothy was 87 when she died, having known the Lord for 60 years. She told me that when she was in her mid-40s, her husband died (after being quite ill for a number of years). Dorothy became a believer when she was in her 20s, but she kept Him on the "backburner" for a long time. After her husband died, the Lord got her attention again. She began praying that He'd give her an insatiable desire for Him and His Word. I met her 40 years later, and she had such a tender heart for the Lord.

She continued to fall more in love with Him right up until she died. She was a great example to me of someone who "pressed on to maturity."

- If you've become "dull of hearing" or you're on the verge of that religious rut, tell the Lord about it.

  "I lack the desire to sit at Your feet."
  "Serving you has become a duty rather than a pleasure."
  "I avoid worship services because I don't like some aspect of the service."
  "I've read the Bible a lot, and I already know what it says, what's the point?"
  "I go to church regularly, isn't that enough?"

- Then, praise Him for His grace and forgiveness. Thank Him for His infinite understanding (Psalm 147:5) and that He already knows all the things you listed above, because He knows everything about you (Psalm 139:1-6). Thank Him for leading you to study Hebrews and for the things you're learning. Then ask Him to refresh your heart and sharpen the dullness. Ask Him to heighten your desire to know Him better and regularly remind you of your Savior. Then "press on to maturity" and cling to Jesus. Ask the Holy Spirit, the Helper, to show you how to grow.

- You might be in a great place with the Lord today. You're enjoying Him and learning and growing in brand-new ways. Enjoy this season of growth, and thank Him for specific things that you're learning about Him. Make it a point throughout your day to thank and praise Him. While you're driving, rather than listening to music or talking on the phone, talk to Him. Share His goodness with your children, your spouse, or your roommate.

- Perhaps you're in a season of suffering. Remember that Jesus Christ is your great High Priest. You can draw near to Him and find comfort and grace, understanding and strength. You can pour out your heart to Him, and He understands your emotional and physical pain—fully and perfectly. "Press on" in the face of pain and cling to Jesus. Ask others to pray for you—don't suffer alone. If you're awake late at night, use that time to pray. If you're in pain, ask the Lord, who suffered terrible pain, to give you strength to endure.

DAY TWO

☐ Read Hebrews

Hebrews 6:4-12

As we've discovered in our study, the audience to whom the author of Hebrews writes (inspired by the Spirit of God) includes believers as well as unbelievers who have yet to take the Gospel seriously or who started well, were part of this band of believers, enjoyed the community of faith, and then turned away from God. For people who fall into this group, there is a stern warning. There also is great encouragement and exhortation to those who love the Lord and serve believers—they are not forgotten by the Lord.

1.   Read Hebrews 6:4-12 in the New Living Translation:

For it is impossible to bring back to repentance those who were once enlightened— those who have experienced the good things of heaven and shared in the Holy Spirit, who have tasted the goodness of the word of God and the power of the age to come and who then turn away from God. It is impossible to bring such people back to repentance; by rejecting the Son of God, they themselves are nailing him to the cross once again and holding him up to public shame.

When the ground soaks up the falling rain and bears a good crop for the farmer, it has God's blessing. But if a field bears thorns and thistles, it is useless. The farmer will soon condemn that field and burn it.

2.   a. According to Hebrews 6:4-6, how does the writer describe "those who were once enlightened?"

b. What's "impossible" according to these verses and why?

c. What's the consequence of "rejecting God?"

Biblical commentator John MacArthur writes, *"Because they believe [this] warning is addressed to Christians, some interpreters hold that the passage teaches that salvation can be lost. If the interpretation were true, however, the passage would also teach that, once lost, salvation could never be regained....But Christians are not being addressed, and it is the opportunity for receiving salvation, not salvation itself, that can be lost."* [2] Remember, Jesus is able to "save forever" those who draw near to Him, and the writer is emphasizing the importance of taking Jesus Christ and His salvation seriously.

Truth Search

3. Hebrews 6:7-8 shows us the Gospel is like the rain that falls on the earth. Compare these two verses with Jesus' words in Matthew 13:24-30, 36-43.

   a. What does the farmer's crop yield?

   b. Who is the landowner/one who sows the seed? What does he tell the slaves to do with the tares?

   c. What do these passages teach about the crop that is good versus that which is useless?

d. Who is responsible for separating the wheat from the tares once the harvest comes?

Jesus uses the agricultural analogy to explain the Biblical principle that there will always be unbelievers in our midst and sometimes even in leadership positions in the church. It isn't our responsibility to sift out the bad from the good. Our responsibility is to look to Jesus and press on to maturity in the power of the Spirit.

4.   How does the "tone" of the passage change in Hebrews 6:9-12 and why?

5.   What do you learn about God and about the people to whom the writer refers?

6.   Hebrews 6:11-12 says, "We want each of you to show this same diligence to the very end, in order to make your hope sure. We do not want you to become lazy, but to imitate those who through faith and patience inherit what has been promised." Once again there's a reminder to "show diligence" and to not "become lazy."

a. Based upon what this says, what is the source of our motivation and why?

b. "Imitate those who through faith and patience inherit the promises" (Hebrews 6:12). "Remember those who led you, who spoke the word of God to you; and considering the outcome of their way of life, imitate their faith" (Hebrews 13:7). Dorothy, who I mentioned earlier, is someone whose faith I seek to imitate. What about you? Describe someone you've known or admired who inspires you. Someone whose faith, patience, and hope you can imitate. Explain why you chose this person.

Reflect & Respond

"He became the Son of Man that we might become the sons of God. He was born in a cattle-shed, reared in obscurity, and lived in poverty. He had neither training nor education. Only once did He ever cross the boundary of His little native land, and even that was in babyhood. Yet His birth set angels singing, and wise men worshipping, and shepherds wondering…Great men have come and gone, yet He lives on. Herod could not kill Him in childhood. Satan could not seduce Him in manhood. Though He voluntarily laid down His life, even death could not destroy Him, and the grave could not hold Him. The past cannot confine Him. He lives in the present, the Contemporary of every generation. He is the only Being in the universe at present with an immortal human body. He is the risen, reigning, returning Lord; and His first coming as Saviour will be crowned by His second coming as Sovereign. He is the ever-living, ever-loving, everlasting Saviour who saves to the uttermost all who come unto God by Him!" [3]

℮ Have you placed your faith in Jesus Christ—the One who is unlike any other? What is keeping you from receiving His gift of salvation? Or, maybe you're ready to accept His death on the cross as payment for your sin. All you need to do is ask. You can pray something like this:

Lord Jesus, I need You. Thank You for dying on the cross and paying for my sin. Thank You for Your forgiveness and for the promise of eternal life. Thank You for initiating a relationship with me. I receive You as my Savior and my Lord.

℮ Is there someone the Lord keeps bringing across your path who needs to hear about Jesus? Spend some time and pray for that person. Pray the Lord will soften his/her heart, and pray you'll step out and open your mouth. Share the good news of salvation in Jesus Christ today.

DAY THREE

DIGGING DEEPER

A favorite book of mine is called *The Jesus Storybook Bible*. I love how the author interprets this amazing story—I wish I could include the illustrations, as well. Today we're just going to read this excerpt and ponder its message. We'll begin in Genesis 12 with Abraham who, by faith, receives God's promise of great blessing. We'll look into his life more in Day Four.

Son of Laughter

God's special promise to Abraham from Genesis 12-21

Years passed and things didn't get any better. People were still just as cruel and mean to one another. They still got sick and died. God's world was still full of tears. It was never meant to be like this.

But God was getting ready to do something about it. He was going to make all the wrong things right, and he was going to do it through...a family.

"Abraham," God said. "How many stars are there?" (God was about to tell his friend a wonderful secret.)

"Let me see," Abraham said, rolling up his sleeves. (But have you ever tried counting stars? Then you know how hard it is.) "992,994,997. Uh-Oh. No. Wait. 1, 2,..." Of course, he kept losing count. "Too many!" he said.

"Guess what!" God laughed. "I will give you so many children and grandchildren and great grandchildren, you won't be able to count them either."

Abraham couldn't help giggling at such a wonderful idea. But he stopped himself. How could he have a family? Don't be silly. He didn't have any children, let alone grandchildren. He wiped away a tear. Anyway it was far too late for him to start having babies at his age, he was 99 years old! What could God mean?

"Abraham," God said. "Believe me."

And then God told Abraham his Secret Rescue Plan. "Abraham, I will make your family very big," God promised. "Until one day, your family will come to number more than even all the stars in the sky."

Abraham looked up at the dark night sky, thick with stars.

"You will be my special family, my people, and through you everyone on earth will be blessed."

It was an incredible promise—God was going to rescue the world through Abraham's family!

One of his great-great-great grandchildren would be the Child, the Promised One, the Rescuer.

"But it's too wonderful!" Abraham said, "How can it be true?"

"Is anything too good to be true?" God asked. "Is anything too wonderful for me?"

So Abraham trusted what God said more than what his eyes could see. And he believed.

Now when Sarah heard God's promise, she just laughed to herself. But it wasn't a happy laugh, it had tears in it. Could she really have a baby when she was 90 years old? No, of course not, don't be silly, it was far too late.

Sarah didn't *believe* God could do what he promised. She had forgotten that when God says something, it's as good as done. (Of course, it was as easy for God to give her a baby as it was for him to make all the stars in the sky.)

Sure enough, nine months later, just as God had promised, Sarah gave birth to a baby boy. They named him Isaac, which means "son of laughter." And Sarah laughed. But this time it was a glorious, happy laugh. Her dream had come true.

God would do as he promised. He would always look after Abraham's family, his special people.

And one day, God would send another baby, a baby promised to a girl who didn't even have a husband. But this baby would bring laughter to the whole world. This baby would *be* everyone's dream come true. [4]

1. As you read this story from a child's viewpoint, what stands out to you as you hear about Abraham, Sarah, and God?

2. Underline all of the references to God, His character, and His promises. Which of these gives you hope and comfort today, and why?

3. What is going on in your life today that requires you to "trust what God [says] more that what [your] eyes can see"?

4. Which of God's promises can you stand on as He calls you to trust?

Reflection

There are so many Psalms that encourage me when I've lost heart and forget that nothing is "too wonderful" for God. Today I read Psalm 116, which the Lord has used to comfort and embolden me on numerous occasions. I include it here because it's a great prayer that mingles desperation (a state I experience quite often) with thankfulness.

☙ Use this Psalm as a guideline for prayer and lay before Him your requests and desire to trust.

> I love the LORD, because He hears
>
> My voice and my supplications.
>
> Because He has inclined His ear to me,
>
> Therefore I shall call upon Him as long as I live.

Thank You, Lord, for hearing my voice and my prayers. Even when I don't know what to say or how to pray, You lean down and listen to my feeble voice. Thank You.

> The cords of death encompassed me
>
> And the terrors of Sheol came upon me;
>
> I found distress and sorrow.
>
> Then I called upon the name of the LORD:
>
> "O LORD, I beseech You, Save my life!"

There are times when my life feels dark, when this situation I'm in feels like it's never going to end. I do feel distressed and sad. Thank You that Your Word reminds me I can call on You. I can implore You to take me out of this situation, to help me, to save me from what's happening.

> Gracious is the LORD, and righteous;
>
> Yes, our God is compassionate.
>
> The LORD preserves the simple;
>
> I was brought low, and He saved me.

☙ Insert your own prayer. Think about the reason the psalmist remembers God's grace, righteousness, and compassion in the midst of feeling distress and sorrow. How might the same attributes encourage you right now?

> Return to your rest, O my soul,
>
> For the LORD has dealt bountifully with you.
>
> For You have rescued my soul from death,
>
> My eyes from tears,
>
> My feet from stumbling.
>
> I shall walk before the LORD
>
> In the land of the living.

@ Why do you think the psalmist is able to consider resting at this point? In what ways has the Lord been bountiful in your life recently, and how does His provision—either emotionally or physically—bring you hope and life?

DAY FOUR

☐ Read Hebrews

Hebrews 6:18-20

God's word is full of promises, one of which the Bible refers to over and over again—His promise to Abraham. "I will surely bless you, I will surely multiply you." Abraham had to walk by faith with diligence and great patience for a long time before he experienced the fulfillment of this promise. Throughout Scripture, whenever Abraham and his faith is mentioned, the focus isn't really on his great faith as much as God's great faithfulness. "God swore an oath on His own death that he would fulfill the promise. Since God is eternally self-existent, it is impossible for Him to die, so the promise is absolutely secure" (Hebrews 6:17-18 NLT).

1. a. Read Hebrews 6:18-20.

    b. Now, go back to the Old Testament and read the following passages in Genesis, and jot down what you learn about God, God's promise, and Abraham.

	<u>God</u>	<u>God's Promise</u>	<u>Abraham</u>
Genesis 12:1-3			
Genesis 15:1-6			

2.   Twenty-five years go by before God blesses Abraham and Sarah with a child—Isaac. We'll look more closely at their journey in a future lesson, but needless to say, 25 years is a long time to wait.

   a. Read Romans 4:18-20, and write down what you discover about Abraham and Sarah. What insight do you gain from this passage into their faith?

   b. What do you learn about God?

3.   a. Now read Genesis 22. Note: by this time Isaac (the child and fulfillment of God's promise) is a young boy.

   b. Describe what God asks of Abraham and Abraham's response in Genesis 22:1-10.

4. Refer back to Hebrews 6:16-18. Then summarize what happens in Genesis 22:11-19. Take special note of Abraham's focus and faith, and God's corresponding provision and oath.

    "God's oath to Abraham is secure not only because He is unable to die, but also because He is unable to lie [two unchangeable things]. God is truth, and all He says and does manifests truth" (Hebrews 6:17-18).

5. How is Jesus, the ultimate fulfillment of that oath, described in Hebrews 6:19-20?

Reflect & Respond

Jesus is our sure and steadfast hope—like an anchor for our souls. What a great word picture. Even when everything else is uncertain, Jesus remains unwavering. Nothing about Him ever changes. The "hope" that the world offers is a "cross-your-fingers-I-hope-I-have-a-good-day" hope—it's circumstantial and shallow. The hope that is ours in Christ never disappoints because it's rooted in His character.

Over the past few weeks, I received two phone calls that demonstrate the hope that is ours in Christ. One friend called to tell me about a serious medical issue that she and her husband were facing with their son. They felt helpless, uncertain, and afraid. They prayed, sought prayer from some friends, and could only cling to Christ. When the situation seemed to reach a place of hopelessness, God intervened, supernaturally. "God is faithful—He answers prayer!" my friend exclaimed. "Tell other people that God answers prayer!"

Another friend called to tell me how she and her husband were helping their daughter look for a new car—hers was on its last leg. You can imagine, I'm sure, that they were discouraged by the high price of new cars. They prayed for guidance and for two days combed new car lots. They persevered and prayed. The third day of their search a "friend of a friend" was selling a car—and, you know the rest of the story. The Lord provided a like-new used car for her daughter. My friend shouted, "Why do we try doing anything without the Lord? He is always faithful to provide." I love these kinds of phone calls.

There are times, lots of times, when the answer isn't "yes." The Lord remains faithful even when it seems like, feels like, and looks like He doesn't care. I have several wonderful friends who long to get married, but the Lord hasn't provided a husband. My husband Bob and I desired to have children and prayed toward that end for many years, and the Lord's answer was "no." He remains sure and steadfast and an anchor for my soul—His goodness and faithfulness is folded into His sovereign plan. I trust His will for our lives. Sure, there are times when I grieve that empty space in my life—I would love to have my own child; yet, I am content with the life to which God has called me. He has used my childlessness to draw me close to Him in ways that I can't describe. For that I'm so thankful.

ⓔ Describe a recent situation when you experienced Jesus as your sure and steadfast hope. Perhaps He provided for you in a significant and surprising way or helped you through a situation that at first seemed hopeless.

ⓔ Perhaps you're facing something very difficult, like my first friend. How does this passage encourage you, and how can you count on God's character in the face of this challenge?

DAY FIVE

Review this week's lesson and continue to read through Hebrews. I hope by now the book is beginning to make more sense. I'm praying for you, as I prepare and write, that you and I will pay close attention to our salvation and our Savior, and we'll press on to maturity with diligence and patience, clinging to Jesus in the power of the Holy Spirit.

Remember my friend Dorothy? As she neared her mid-80s, she was asked to co-lead a women's Bible study group. In an effort to be well prepared, she completely renovated her study space. She went from reading her Bible in a soft and cozy recliner to sitting at a desk surrounded by a variety of study tools. I so admired her willingness to "press on to maturity." Dorothy didn't just "coast" into heaven; she stepped into the presence of the Lord spiritually fresh and vibrant.

Here are some suggestions to help you encounter the Savior:

1. I believe that we partner with the Lord Jesus in our growth—we need to abide in Him, and He'll bring about the fruit. No matter where you are in your journey with Him, take some time and evaluate.

2. How are you positioning yourself to grow and mature in Christ? Maybe all you need to do is renovate your study space like Dorothy did. I have a friend who designates a spot in her backyard for prayer. Maybe you can clear away a spot in your bedroom or basement that is reserved for you and the Lord.

3. If you're just beginning to walk with the Lord, then I encourage you to set aside time to read and pray…even if you start simply by spending 15 minutes reading Hebrews and doing a few questions from this study.

4. If you've been a believer for a longer period of time, don't get comfortable. Pursue Jesus through His Word. Read other books that challenge your thinking and get you into the Word in a fresh way. I love to read. Often I'll read a chapter from an outside source along with reading my Bible. Take a seminary course on Spiritual Disciplines or another topic of interest. There are all kinds of resources online that can enhance your pursuit of Christ. Get some ideas from someone you trust who knows which resources are biblically sound and Christ centered.

5. Read through the Bible, and look for God's grace as you do. Just a few years ago, every time I came across a passage describing God's grace, I'd mark it. It was fun to watch as God demonstrated His favor throughout the whole Bible.

6. Determine in your heart, no matter where you are in the journey, to seek Him with a whole heart all of your days. You'll go through seasons when time is sparse—that's ok. You'll also go through seasons when you have more time. Ask Him to help you in your pursuit. If this week's lesson has challenged you to take the Lord more seriously, write down a prayer of commitment and mark today as a point in your journey when you determined to press on to maturity.

Wherever you are along the path of maturity and growth, remember that it's not about you, and it's all about Him. He made it possible for you and me to have a vital, growing relationship with Him at the cross. He delights in, loves, and longs for intimate communion with you and me. With this in mind, I include an excerpt from *The Jesus Storybook Bible* that wraps up, quite well, this week's study.

It picks up in Genesis 22:11-19 after God provided a ram to take the place of Isaac (Abraham's son) on the altar.

And as they sat there on the mountaintop, watching the embers of the fire die in the cool night air, the stars above them sparkling in the velvet sky, God helped Abraham and Isaac understand something. God wanted his people to live, not die. God wanted to rescue his people, not punish them. But they must trust him.

"One day Someone will be born into your family," God promised them. "And he will bring happiness to the whole world."

God was getting ready to give the whole world a wonderful present. It would be God's way to tell his people, "I love you."

Many years later, another Son would climb another hill, carrying wood on his back. Like Isaac, he would trust his father and do what his father asked. He wouldn't struggle or run away.

Who was he? God's Son, his only Son—the Son he loved.

The Lamb of God. [5]

1 Ray Stedman, Commentary on Hebrews (Online)

2 John MacArthur, *The MacArthur Bible Commentary Hebrews* (Chicago: Moody Bible Institute, 1983),p. 146.

3 J. Sidlow Baxter. *Going Deeper* (Grand Rapids: Zondervan, 1971) pp. 108-109.

4 Sally Lloyd-Jones. *The Jesus Storybook Bible* (Grand Rapids: Zondervan, 2007) pp.55-60.

5 Ibid, p.69.

Jesus, Our Priest & King

Hebrews 8:1-10:39

The phrase that strikes me the most in this section of our study is found in Hebrews 9:1, "Now even the first covenant had regulations of divine worship and the earthly sanctuary." The first covenant had regulations of divine worship—lots of them, and the sanctuary was earthly. Let's step back and consider some of what we've learned so far from Hebrews.

Jesus Christ passed through the heavens and became our Great High Priest. Because of His absolute perfection He is able to "save forever those who draw near to God through Him." No longer do we have to follow strict guidelines and rigid regulations in order to worship the Holy God, no longer do we need to offer sacrifices for our sin year after year. Because of Jesus Christ we can worship God in spirit and in truth.

Right from the beginning, God has pointed toward Jesus Christ. His divine "rescue plan" was set into place in the Garden and continued with the inception of the Law, the priesthood, and the tabernacle, all of which were a "copy" or "shadow" of the amazing things to come.

The result? Today, you and I, because of Jesus Christ's shed blood, can enter the Most Holy Place anytime day or night, anywhere—at home in our kitchen or in the desert of Afghanistan. No longer is the place of worship earthly; it is heavenly and spiritual. Believers in Jesus Christ are His holy temples because He did what we never could—paid the penalty for sins, once for all.

Worship Jesus Christ right where you are—propped against a pillow on your bed, sitting in a coffee shop, or on an airplane—and praise Him for being our great "high priest, who has taken His seat at the right hand of the throne of the Majesty in the heavens...." Praise Him for saving us forever, for cleansing our conscience from dead works, and for calling us to serve the living God.

DAY ONE

☐ Read Hebrews

Hebrews 8:1-3

When doing a study like this, it's easy to lose "the forest for the trees." We've looked at a lot of details surrounding the Law and the priesthood. In this week's lesson, we'll continue to look at some of the important points regarding the tabernacle. Sometimes it really helps to step back and remember the big picture and the purpose behind the details. So, today we'll do just that: take a step back and remind ourselves what Hebrews is all about; as we do, pray for God's guidance: "Your hands made me and formed me; give me understanding to learn Your [Word]" (Psalm 119:73 NASB).

1. Read Hebrews 8:1-3 in the NIV:

    "The point of what we are saying is this: We do have such a high priest, who sat down at the right hand of the throne of the Majesty in heaven, and who serves in the sanctuary, the true tabernacle set up by the Lord, not by man.

    Every high priest is appointed to offer both gifts and sacrifices, and so it was necessary for this one also to have something to offer. If he were on earth, he would not be a priest, for there are already men who offer the gifts prescribed by the law. They serve at a sanctuary that is a copy and shadow of what is in heaven. This is why Moses was warned when he was about to build the tabernacle: 'See to it that you make everything according to the pattern shown you on the mountain.' But the ministry Jesus has received is as superior to theirs as the covenant of which he is mediator is superior to the old one, and it is founded on better promises."

2. a. According to Hebrews 8:1-2, what is the main point of what we've been studying, and why do you think the recipients of this letter needed this reminder?

    b. Why do we need this reminder today?

3. The following questions are for review and for the purpose of honing in on the main point: "We do have such a high priest, who sat down at the right hand of the throne of the Majesty in heaven, and who serves in the sanctuary, the true tabernacle set up by the Lord, not by man." Use Hebrews 8:1-5 and other passages in Hebrews for your answers.

    a. What is the gift that Jesus, our great High Priest, offered, and why was it superior to the gifts and sacrifices offered by earthly priests?

    b. If Jesus was on earth, why would He not be a priest, and what makes Jesus superior to all of the other priests?

4. Again, for review, summarize the difference between the old covenant and the new.

5. One of the implications of the new covenant is that it includes not only Israel but also "Gentiles" (anyone who isn't a Jew). It's important to recognize where Gentiles stood before God apart from Christ. Read Ephesians 2:11-22 and answer the following questions.

    a. What was true of Gentiles (Ephesians 2:11-12)?

b. According to Ephesians 2:13-18, what things were accomplished by "the blood of Christ?"

c. Read Ephesians 2:19-22 and summarize what is now true of Gentiles.

6. a. What insight does this passage in Ephesians give you as you consider the new covenant?

b. Was there something in particular in this passage that meant a lot to you personally?

Reflect & Respond

There is a tendency to allow our study of Hebrews to stimulate our brains rather than our hearts. There are so many theological truths, historical facts, and technical details that we could not only miss the forest for the trees, but we might miss the love and grace of Jesus that flows through the Old and New Testament (as we've seen so clearly in Hebrews). We might overlook the fact that God's loving and sacrificial plan of redemption has been in place since Adam and Eve, and that its message affects all people everywhere for eternity.

     © Step back and look at the big picture of God's plan and allow the truth of His sovereignty to sink into your soul. How does it make you feel to know that He, the Sovereign One, set in motion a "rescue plan" thousands of years ago that involves you?

     © Reflect back over Ephesians 2:11-22 and meditate on what it means to you personally to know that you've been brought near to Christ—after being separate from Him, alone and without hope, a stranger to His promises. As you do this, insert your name into the text and marvel at what God, through Christ's blood, has done for you.

     © What difference does it make to know that you're no longer alone and that you have hope?

     © Think for a moment about the non-Christians you encounter on a regular basis, like your dental hygienist, a hair stylist, a lab partner, or a co-worker. Often we see these people more frequently than we do some of our closest friends. Have you considered God may have you in their lives for a reason? This week take the opportunity to share with one of the non-believers in your life about your relationship with the Lord. You could use your study of Hebrews as a springboard for conversation. Tell someone about God's "rescue plan," and how it started all the way back in Genesis. Tell someone how God rescued you from sin and promised you eternal life.

DAY TWO

☐ Read Hebrews

Hebrews 9:1-10

In Exodus 25:8, God tells Moses, "And let them construct a sanctuary for Me, that I may dwell among them." The children of Israel sinned against God countless times, but He still desired to dwell among His people. They rebelled again and again, and each time God relented and forgave their sin. Throughout history God has shown mercy and grace to sinful man, and also throughout history His "rescue plan" has been in place and is now fully revealed in Jesus Christ.

1. Read Deuteronomy 9-10:11 for historical background. Pay close attention to and write down the adjectives used to describe the children of Israel (9:6, 13, 22, 26-27).

2. Look carefully at Deuteronomy 10:12-22. What does this passage reveal about God?

3. Read Hebrews 9:1-10 in the New Living Translation:
    "That first covenant between God and Israel had regulations for worship and a place of worship here on earth. There were two rooms in that Tabernacle. In the first room were a lampstand, a table, and sacred loaves of bread on the table. This room was called the Holy Place. Then there was a curtain, and behind the curtain was the second room called the Most Holy Place. In that room were a gold incense altar and a wooden chest called the Ark of the Covenant, which was covered with gold on all sides. Inside the Ark were a gold jar containing manna, Aaron's staff

that sprouted leaves, and the stone tablets of the covenant. Above the Ark were the cherubim of divine glory, whose wings stretched out over the Ark's cover, the place of atonement. But we cannot explain these things in detail now.

When these things were all in place, the priests regularly entered the first room as they performed their religious duties. But only the high priest ever entered the Most Holy Place, and only once a year. And he always offered blood for his own sins and for the sins the people had committed in ignorance. By these regulations the Holy Spirit revealed that the entrance to the Most Holy Place was not freely open as long as the Tabernacle and the system it represented were still in use.

This is an illustration pointing to the present time. For the gifts and sacrifices that the priests offer are not able to cleanse the consciences of the people who bring them. For that old system deals only with food and drink and various cleansing ceremonies—physical regulations that were in effect only until a better system could be established" (NLT).

4. This passage also reveals some details about the earthly tent—the tabernacle (There is much more detail in Exodus 25-40.). The outer one, we learn, is where the lampstand and the table and the sacred bread were kept—the Holy Place. Read the following for insight into the purpose of the Holy Place, and write down your discoveries.

    Hebrews 9:6

    Hebrews 9:7-10

According to this passage, no gift or offering can make the worshiper perfect in conscience. In other words, the cleansing was outward and could do nothing for a guilty conscience. Commentator John Piper writes: *"As a foreshadowing of Christ, God counted the blood of the animals as sufficient for cleansing the flesh—the ceremonial uncleanness, but not the conscience....Our conscience condemns us. We don't feel good enough to come to God. And no matter how distorted our consciences are, this much is true: We are not good enough to come to him....The only answer in these modern times, as in all other times, is the blood of Christ. When our conscience rises up and condemns us, where will we turn? We turn to Christ. We turn to the suffering and death of Christ—the blood of Christ. This is the only cleansing agent in the universe that gives the conscience relief in life and peace in death."* [1]

5.   Describe a time when your conscience experienced this "relief" that Piper describes.

Something that I really appreciate about walking with Christ is that He lets me know when I sin. My "guilty conscience" almost always is a result of a specific action or attitude. As a matter of fact, today my conscience (prodded by the Spirit) was bothering me. One of my co-workers sent me an e-mail that made me "bristle" and provoked a defensive response, and it wasn't the first time. I knew I was dealing with pride—the Spirit made that very clear. So, I confessed my sin to the Lord and then spent some time looking at some passages that addressed my attitude as well as the attitude that would most honor Him. It is so encouraging to know the Lord will show us the areas we need to surrender to Him and give us the power to respond in humility.

6.   Behind the second veil, there is another tent, which is called the Most Holy Place. In this place, there's the golden altar of incense and the Ark of the Covenant, in which was a golden jar holding manna (a sacred way to remember God's provision in the wilderness); Aaron's rod; and the tablets, on which were written the Ten Commandments; and holy angels overshadowed the mercy seat above the ark.

   Read Hebrews 9:7. What do you learn about the Most Holy Place and those who enter it?

7.   Read Hebrews 9:11-14 in the New Living Translation:
   "So Christ has now become the High Priest over all the good things that have come. He has entered that greater, more perfect Tabernacle in heaven, which was not made by human hands and is not part of this created world. With his own blood—not the blood of goats and calves—he entered the Most Holy Place once for all time and secured our redemption forever.

   Under the old system, the blood of goats and bulls and the ashes of a young cow could cleanse people's bodies from ceremonial impurity. Just think how much more the blood of Christ will purify our consciences from sinful deeds so that we can worship the living God. For by the power of the eternal Spirit, Christ offered himself to God as a perfect sacrifice for our sins" (NLT).

8. According to Hebrews 9:11-14, what makes Jesus Christ's sacrifice superior?

9. Continue reading Hebrews 9:15-22 in the New Living Translation:

> *"That is why he is the one who mediates a new covenant between God and people, so that all who are called can receive the eternal inheritance God has promised them. For Christ died to set them free from the penalty of the sins they had committed under that first covenant.*
>
> *Now when someone leaves a will, it is necessary to prove that the person who made it is dead. The will goes into effect only after the person's death. While the person who made it is still alive, the will cannot be put into effect.*
>
> *That is why even the first covenant was put into effect with the blood of an animal. For after Moses had read each of God's commandments to all the people, he took the blood of calves and goats, along with water, and sprinkled both the book of God's law and all the people, using hyssop branches and scarlet wool. Then he said, "This blood confirms the covenant God has made with you." And in the same way, he sprinkled blood on the Tabernacle and on everything used for worship. In fact, according to the law of Moses, nearly everything was purified with blood. For without the shedding of blood, there is no forgiveness"* (NLT).

The details mentioned in Hebrews 9:18-22 are found in Exodus 40 when Moses performed this act of worship and consecration—thousands of years ago. We now can see clearly why they were a shadow of what's been fulfilled in Christ—He has removed sin by His own death. "When Christ came into the world 1,400 years later, it was more fully revealed that this 'pattern' for the old tabernacle was a copy or a shadow of realities in heaven. The tabernacle was an earthly figure of a heavenly reality…So, all the worship practices of Israel in the Old Testament point toward something more real. Just as there were holy rooms in the tabernacle, where the priests repeatedly took the blood of the animal sacrifices and met with God, so there are infinitely superior 'holy places,' as it were, in heaven, where Christ entered with his own blood, not repeatedly, but once for all." [2]

Reflect & Respond

Hebrews 9:23-28 goes on to say, *"That is why the Tabernacle and everything in it, which were copies of things in heaven, had to be purified by the blood of animals. But the real things in heaven had to be purified with far better sacrifices than the blood of animals. For Christ did not enter into a holy place made with human hands, which was only a copy of the true one in heaven. He entered into heaven itself to appear now before God on our behalf. And he did not enter heaven to offer himself again and again, like the high priest here on earth who enters the Most Holy Place year after year with the blood of an animal. If that had been necessary, Christ would have had to die again and again, ever since the world began. But now, once for all time, he has appeared at the end of the age to remove sin by his own death as a sacrifice"* (NLT).

ⓔ Remember in Hebrews 7:25 we learned that Jesus is our Advocate. He stands before God on our behalf. Here in Hebrews 9:24 it says that He entered into heaven to appear in the presence of God for us. Why do we need Christ to stand in God's presence for us, and why is He the perfect person to do so?

ⓔ What have you learned about Jesus so far that makes you stand in awe, and why?

DAY THREE

DIGGING DEEPER

A recurring theme in Hebrews is eternity. Throughout the book, the writer alludes to the days that are coming. This reminds me that Jesus talked a lot about His kingdom that's to come. Because we live in a temporal world, it's difficult to remember and find hope in something eternal and heavenly. Yet, the topic of God's heavenly kingdom and our eternal hope is a recurring theme throughout the entire Bible. Today we're going to take a brief look at some of the passages in Hebrews and other places in the Bible that give us a window into the future and our future hope.

Pray for a minute and ask the Lord to give you some uninterrupted time with Him. Ask Him to open your eyes to the future hope that is yours in Christ.

1. Let's look at Hebrews and see what's there regarding our future and heaven. Notice as you scan that even back in the Old Testament followers of God knew that something better, something heavenly awaited them. Look at the following and write down what you discover.
    Hebrews 10:37

    Hebrews 11:14-16

    Hebrews 12:26-28

Truth Search

2. Compare these verses with others in the Bible, and write down your discoveries.

    a. The following gives a physical description of what's to come:
       II Peter 3:13

Revelation 21:1 (for more details read 21:10-27)

b. The following give us an emotional and relational picture of what's to come:
Revelation 21:3-8

Revelation 22:3-5

c. The following give us a picture of Jesus as our Priest and King:
Revelation 21:5-6

Revelation 22:16

3. Recently I was with a friend, and we were talking about the current state of the world, which we agreed isn't very good. She made a comment that has stuck with me. She reminded me that the turmoil and upheaval we hear about every day is exactly what Jesus said would happen. He said that wars and rumors of wars, trials and tribulations would increase before He returns the second time (Matthew 24:3-14). What do the following verses remind us to do while we wait for His return?
II Peter 3:11-13; 17-18

I John 2:28-3:3

Revelation 22:7

4. Look closely at Hebrews 8:11-12. According to these verses, what does the future hold because of the New Covenant?

Reflect & Respond

I write these questions knowing full well that I don't know very much about heaven or the New Earth that's to come. Nor can I begin to imagine what it's like to live in the presence of God. Nevertheless, I can't help but think it's amazing. I wonder if once we're all there, we'll understand the meaning of "awesome." It's strange and wonderful how we walk with a God we can't see; we experience His presence, hear His voice, and follow His lead. We've been given His mind in order to understand His depths (I Corinthians 2:10-16), and we look forward to a brand-new place to live even after we die. Whether or not we completely understand what's to come, we can press on and lay hold of our hope until that day comes.

I conclude today with a quote from *Things Unseen* by Mark Buchanan (a favorite author of mine).

> *"So how can there be no more sorrow in heaven? What is the 'old order of things' that passes away? Is it that our memories themselves are erased and that all the pain that ambushed us and all the joy that fled us on earth, all the wrong we've done and had done to us, simply slip into a vast sea of forgetting? Or is it that we get divine perspective on all those things, with God's transcendent power and consoling depths of understanding—an 'aha, so that's what God was up to' revelation?...*
>
> *Heaven is where our inescapable sense of loss and incompleteness is overcome. It is the one thing large enough to answer our deepest longing and console our deepest griefs [sic]. Our hunger for perfect justice and perfect mercy and perfect joy and perfect peace—all is met there."* [3]

◎ Life is painful, joy is often fleeting, and the battle against our flesh and the devil is fierce. How can thoughts of a new heaven and new earth really bring perspective in the midst of our fiery trials?

DAY FOUR

☐ Read Hebrews

Hebrews 10:19-25; 32-39

In a few months I will celebrate my 49th birthday. I figure from the time I was born, I have taken a bath or shower thousands of times. There's nothing quite as refreshing and revitalizing as a good, hot sudsy shower. It rejuvenates, revitalizes, and soothes. However, no matter how floral or spicy the shower gel or powerful the deodorant soap, I cannot stay clean and fresh without a bath at least every few days. And, neither can you.

The Jewish sacrificial system was a lot like taking a bath—only certainly more serious. No amount of sacrifice could cleanse a conscience or take away sin for a priest or the common person. I can't help but think about what it was like to be reminded of my sin over and over again, to constantly seek out cleansing and rest and never find it.

The Gospel is such a contrast to the old covenant because the price Jesus Christ paid was the ultimate sacrifice.

1. Let's take a walk through Hebrews and review what we've discovered about Jesus and the gift of forgiveness. Jot down your observations.

    Hebrews 1:3

    Hebrews 2:9

    Hebrews 5:8-9

    Hebrews 7:25

    Hebrews 9:14

Hebrews 10:12

Hebrews 10:18

2. As you reflect on what you've discovered, how does the gift of forgiveness affect you personally, and why?

3. Read Hebrews 10:19-25. Now that we may confidently enter into the very presence of God, because of our great High Priest Jesus, how are we exhorted to respond?
   Hebrews 10:22

   Hebrews 10:23

   Hebrews 10:24-25

4. Which response is important to you now, and which do you need to integrate into your life?

It's so important to remember that drawing near, holding fast, and assembling together aren't choices we make once and then we're done. Nor are they always easy. Sometimes we forget, sometimes we lose heart. John Piper writes, "Being sanctified means that we are imperfect and in process. We are becoming holy—but are not yet fully holy. And it is precisely these—and only these—who are already perfected. The joyful encouragement here is that the evidence of our perfection before God is not our experienced perfection, but our experienced progress. The good news is that being on the way is proof that we have arrived." [4]

5. a. Once again, the writer of Hebrews inserts a strong warning to those who are listening (maybe even halfheartedly) out on the fringes. According to Hebrews 10:26-30, what is the person who deserves judgment described as doing?

    b. Why, based upon all that you've learned so far, is there a more severe punishment for those who "trample underfoot the Son of God"?

Remember, it's only by the grace of God that we escape His judgment. Romans 5:8-9 (NASB) says, *"But God demonstrates His own love toward us, in that while we were yet sinners, Christ died for us. Much more then, having now been justified by His blood, we shall be saved from the wrath of God through Him."*

Recently I had the opportunity to share the gospel with several Italian college students who have been raised around "religion" all of their lives. Upon hearing these verses, several said to me, "I've never heard of a love like this before." That's what makes Jesus Christ's sacrifice superior to every other sacrifice offered. It's a demonstration of His love, God's love, which is undeserved and unconditional. If you know Jesus Christ as your Savior, you will not fall under His punishment—Christ bore the weight of His wrath at the cross. You never need to be terrified of God, because His love has been "poured out within our hearts" (Romans 5:5).

6. a. Read Hebrews 10:32-39. Like in previous chapters, the writer shifts his attention from those who need warning to those who believe in Jesus. How does he describe this group?

    b. "Don't throw away your confidence, which has a great reward. Therefore, you have need of endurance so that when you have done the will of God, you may receive what was promised" (Hebrews 10:35-36). What is the promise in Hebrews 10:37-38?

Reflect & Respond

As I write this lesson, I'm encouraged. Lately following Christ and holding fast my confidence in Him has felt hard. Different situations I'm facing make me want to "quit" sometimes. I need to remember Jesus, remember that He is the source of my confidence and freedom. He will give me the strength to persevere until He comes again. I'm so grateful I can take my problems, my worries, and my woes to His throne of grace and find help. I do find comfort and hope in the promise that "He who is coming will not delay." And until He comes, He is present with me always. His Spirit is my helper and my guide.

ⓒ What about you? What's going on in your life that feels endless? Why do you think we need confidence and endurance to do the will of God?

ⓒ Is there something about Him from our study that helps you endure?

◎ Write out a prayer to the Lord, requesting help in your particular time of need.

DAY FIVE

☐ Read Hebrews

Once again, this is a good day to catch up on your Hebrews reading and the week's lesson. I know that we're covering a lot of ground, and you're absorbing a lot of information (at least I hope it's sinking in). Remember: Hebrews is a large and complex book of Scripture. There are days when I feel like I'm trudging through and making little progress in my understanding. I really do take great encouragement in the fact that God is the source of wisdom and the things of the Spirit.

Take a minute as you wrap up this week and read II Corinthians 2:10-16 (I referred to it earlier in the lesson.). Read it aloud and ponder what it says. We have the mind of Christ, and because His Spirit lives in us, we have the ability to grasp the depths of God. The writer of Hebrews also alludes to this when he calls us to press on to maturity.

Rest in the fact that the Holy Spirit is your teacher. Thank Him and ask Him to help you respond to Him and His Word with a soft and obedient heart. He will show you the areas of your life that need His attention. Draw near to Him and He will draw near to you—He promises.

Finally, as we finish this week's lesson, read this excerpt from the children's book *The Last Battle* by C.S. Lewis:

"And as He spoke He no longer looked to them like a lion; but the things that began to happen after that were so great and beautiful that I cannot write them. And for us this is the end of all the stories, and we can most truly say that they all lived happily ever after.

But for them it was only the beginning of the real story. All their life in this world and all their adventures in Narnia had only been the cover and the title page: now at last they were beginning Chapter One of the Great Story which no one on earth has read: which goes on forever: in which every chapter is better than the one before." [5]

For Further Study

God is holy—He is perfectly righteous and just, without sin or stain. Only God is holy, which is why we need Jesus, the perfect and holy sacrifice for our sin. He is perfect man and perfect God.

- Read the following verses to learn more about our holy God. In light of all that we've learned so far in Hebrews, how do these verses help you understand His holiness?

    I Samuel 2:2

    Psalm 77:13

    Isaiah 54:5

    Revelation 4:8

1 John Piper, *The Passion of Jesus Christ*. (Wheaton: Crossway Books, 2004) pp. 50-51.

2 Ibid, page 67.

3 Mark Buchanan. *Things Unseen*. (Sisters: Multnomah Press, 2002), page 87.

4 John Piper. *The Passion of Jesus Christ*. (Wheaton: Crossway Books, 2004), page 49.

5 C.S. Lewis. *The Last Battle* (New York City: HarperCollins, 1994)

LESSON NINE

Pause to Enjoy

Today I'm propped up against a pillow at the Pine Cone Inn located in South Lake Tahoe. I am on the staff of a Christian ministry called Campus Crusade for Christ, and my husband, Bob, and I are visiting a "Summer Project" being run by 70 college students from around the United States. During the day, they work all over town at places like Quiznos, Cold Stone Creamery, and Kentucky Fried Chicken, and at night, they learn a variety of ministry skills, study the Word, and pray and worship together. Throughout the week, they take the initiative to share the Gospel with co-workers and tourists. It's always so encouraging to hear about the lives that are transformed by Christ every summer—both on and off the project. After 10 weeks of intense ministry, they go back to school and put into practice what they've learned over the summer in Lake Tahoe.

Every time we drive from Reno into beautiful South Lake Tahoe, I am struck by the contrast. Dusty, dry, barren desert is gradually replaced by dense, emerald forests of towering pine. As we make the steady incline, the flat landscape is replaced by snowcapped mountains. As we near the town, the tightly packed trees periodically open a window to an enormous lake, but because there are so many trees along the way, it's easy to miss even though Lake Tahoe is huge. When I pay attention and catch an open "window," I marvel at the amazingly blue water. Turquoise, sapphire, cobalt, and indigo extend as far as my eye can see. And then, abruptly, the window closes and I wait for another peek. It's like this until we make our way into town when it's finally in full view.

Well, in Lesson 8, I mentioned a few times the need to pull back and look at the big picture so we don't miss the forest for the trees. We need to remember the "main point": Jesus, our great High Priest, now sits at the right hand of the Majesty in the heavens. In the same way, we don't want to miss some of the rich nuggets that might pass us by as we breeze through Hebrews. So this week, we're going to look at what it means to experience God's forgiveness moment by moment, and what it means to be "eternally secure" in Christ.

In addition, now that we have Hebrews 5-10 under our belt, we're going to do a quick review of Hebrews 1-4. You'll understand why as we go. Just so you know, the format for this lesson will look different from the others.

So, take a deep breath and let it out, sit back and enjoy the scenery—there's something beautiful just around the bend.

DAY ONE

Assurance

The Hebrew audience to which the author writes is a mixture of believers and unbelievers who are experiencing all kinds of persecution under the rule of Nero. Many believers are tempted to turn away from Jesus and return to the Jewish system of rules and rituals. The writer takes great pains to make sure Jesus Christ is exalted, everyone recognizes He is God, and He is superior to the old way of doing things. He also extends strong warnings to those who don't take Christ seriously and neglect the salvation offered to them in Christ and take advantage of the blessings in Christ without making a commitment to Him. These warnings can cause us to wonder if we can lose our salvation, but when that temptation to doubt rises in our hearts, we need to look to Jesus and remember who He is and what He did at the cross. "Hence, also, He is able to save forever those who draw near to God through Him, since He always lives to make intercession for them" (Hebrews 7:25). Our confidence in salvation rests not on our works or our abilities, but on Jesus Christ, who offered up Himself as the perfect sacrifice. The writer of Hebrews, sensitive to the fact that there were unbelievers in their midst, continues to set forth the seriousness and importance of receiving Christ's gift of grace—it's not to be taken lightly.

Today's study gives us the opportunity to enjoy the promise of forgiveness and eternal life and also grasp afresh the reality of who Jesus is and what He did. I'm grateful to have the background of Hebrews 1-10 to enhance and solidify this truth reserved for God's children. I'm also struck by the fact that not everyone knows Jesus like we do. We often have the opportunity to share this Gospel—let's pray that this lesson will encourage us so much that we'll eagerly tell others about our Savior.

1.   a. Read and write out I John 5:11-14.

      b. What has God given us?

c. Who has eternal life and who doesn't?

d. What must we do to have eternal life, and how do we know that we have it (I John 5:13)?

e. What is the basis for our confidence, according to I John 5:14?

2. a. The following verses provide further assurance. Read and write them out below. As you write, note this guarantee rests not in what we do but in the person of Jesus Christ.
John 10:27-29

I Peter 1:3-5

Hebrews 13:5-6

b. Which of the verses/passages above encourage you personally, and why?

3. We looked at Romans 8:31-39 in a previous lesson. Let's take a look again in the New Living Translation:

What shall we say about such wonderful things as these? If God is for us, who can ever be against us? Since he did not spare even his own Son but gave him up for us all, won't he also give us everything else? Who dares accuse us whom God has chosen for his own? No one—for God himself has given us right standing with himself. Who then will condemn us? No one—for Christ Jesus died for us and was raised to life for us, and he is sitting in the place of honor at God's right hand, pleading for us.

Can anything ever separate us from Christ's love? Does it mean he no longer loves us if we have trouble or calamity, or are persecuted, or hungry, or destitute, or in danger, or threatened with death? (As the Scriptures say, "For your sake we are killed every day; we are being slaughtered like sheep.") No, despite all these things, overwhelming victory is ours through Christ, who loved us. And I am convinced that nothing can ever separate us from God's love. Neither death nor life, neither angels nor demons, neither our fears for today nor our worries about tomorrow— not even the powers of hell can separate us from God's love. No power in the sky above or in the earth below—indeed, nothing in all creation will ever be able to separate us from the love of God that is revealed in Christ Jesus our Lord.

a. Romans 8:31 says, "God is for us." According Romans 8:32-34, what does that mean?

b. Perhaps your friends accuse you of needing a "crutch" or family members condemn you for being a follower of Christ. Maybe you hear lies in your head that accuse you of being unworthy of God's love and condemn you for being worthless and a waste of God's time. What does this passage teach you with regard to accusation and condemnation?

c. According to Romans 8:35-37, can anything separate you from God's love? Why or why not?

4. a. Walk through Romans 8:35, and if there is something you're currently experiencing that falls into those categories, write it down. Then, thank God and praise Him that no matter how dark or lonely or hard—nothing—absolutely nothing—can separate you from His Love. *Trouble:* My health is declining, and I'm afraid.

Calamity: We've run out of money and have to declare bankruptcy.

Persecution

Hunger

Being destitute

Danger

Threats

Death

b. According to Romans 8:39, who is the basis for our confidence?

5. This passage is such a great reminder of God's love and generous grace. God most often uses the times when I am troubled by relationships or feel threatened by circumstances to teach me about His love and grace. I would never grasp the security of His love and grace without being forced to run into His arms. With this passage in mind, how has God shown you His love through your most difficult trials?

Reflect & Respond

Ⓒ Write out a "psalm" (poem of praise) expressing your feelings of gratitude. In your own words praise God for being on your side even when everything else seems against you.

DAY TWO

How To Experience God's Love & Forgiveness

God's love and forgiveness is something that is foundational for a new believer and increasingly profound for those who have known the Lord for a while. When I was a brand-new believer, I remember the first time I heard all of my sins were paid for and forgiven—past, present, and future—at the cross. I was so relieved. A few years later, while sharing the same thing with another new believer, I realized in a whole new way that ALL of my sins were forgiven—past, present, and future—at the cross. I didn't hear something new, I just heard it in a whole new way.

As the years have passed, and I've walked with the Lord for a few decades, it never ceases to amaze me how quickly I can lose sight of His grace and forgiveness. Sin surprises me—I don't think I should struggle with "that" anymore. I'll carry the ball and chain of guilt and forget that Jesus cut the chain and set me free. He doesn't remember my sin, so why should I? Horrid pictures will flit into my mind, and I'll feel shame. For a time I even pretend I never had the thought (If I were really a "good Christian," I wouldn't have those thoughts"). Then, I'll find freedom when I confess them to Jesus and remember: "That's why I need a Savior."

Not so long ago, I told some young women the war between my flesh and His Spirit doesn't end by a certain age but continues and perhaps intensifies. I don't struggle with as many "outward" sins as I did when I was a new Christian, but I do battle with envy, pride, jealousy, idolatry, bigotry, malice, gossip.... Every day my flesh rears its ugly head, and every day I have a choice to make: Will I recognize my need for Jesus and His power and yield to Him, or will I wallow in a pool of self-centeredness? The beauty of following Jesus is that He loves me just the same.

The Bible teaches that God is "mindful that we are but dust" (Psalm 103:18). We need Him, desperately, every day to help us through.

1.   a. Define *forgiveness* using a dictionary or www.dictionary.com:

     b. Describe what it means to "be forgiven"?

2.   What keeps you from experiencing God's forgiveness?

3.   a. In Lesson 8, we reviewed Hebrews 1-10 and wrote down every verse that referred to Christ's forgiveness. Go back and refresh your memory (Lesson 8, Day 4, question 1).

b. As you looked, were there verses that touched your heart more than others? If so, why?

Truth Search

4.   Let's compare Hebrews with other passages. Read the following and write down what you observe.

a. Romans 5:6-10
What was true of you before Christ?

What did He do for you?

How can the truth of this passage encourage you throughout each day?

b. Ephesians 2:1-9
What was true of you before Christ?

What did He do for you?

How can the truth of this passage encourage you throughout each day?

c. Colossians 2:13-14
What was true of you before Christ?

What did He do for you?

How can the truth of this passage encourage you throughout each day?

5.   a. Draw out a straight line. Somewhere along that line, draw a cross, which represents Christ's
       death on the cross. To the right of the cross make a mark with the year you were born. To
       the right of that mark make another with the year you received Christ. How many of your
       sins were in the future when Christ died for you? It's a great picture of the fact that ALL of
       your sins were in the future when Christ paid the price once for all. He was victorious over
       sin and death because He is God. We are victorious over sin and death, too, because He is
       our Savior.

b. Has today's lesson enhanced your understanding of God's forgiveness? If so, how?

Reflect & Respond

We can experience this victory all of the time by confessing our sin. First John 1:9 says, "If we confess our sins, He is faithful and righteous to forgive us our sin and to cleanse us from all unrighteousness." To confess means to agree with God about our sin—every time we sin. Years ago I learned to:

- Call it sin (agree with Him about your sin).

- Call it forgiven (thank Him for His gift).

- Call on God to make the change (thank Him for His Spirit who lives in you).

If you're carrying a load of sin around and you're not sure you're forgiven, make a list of those sins on a separate piece of paper. Then write I John 1:9 across the list: Call it sin, call it forgiven, call on God to change you. Rip the list into tiny pieces and throw it away. Rejoice that you're forgiven.

© At the beginning of today's lesson I asked the question, "What keeps you from experiencing God's forgiveness?" Based upon what you've learned today, will you answer that question differently? Why or why not?

DAY THREE

Digging Deeper

"The Cross is the blazing fire at which the flame of our love is kindled, but we have to get near enough for its sparks to fall on us." [1]

I read this quote in a little book called *Living The Cross Centered Life*. The author writes, "That's why our attention must continually be drawn back to what John Stott calls, 'that great and most glorious of all subjects—the cross of Christ.' In the Scriptures we discover a profound urgency for focusing all we are and everything we do around the gospel of the cross." [2]

We're going to draw near to the cross through a powerful passage in Isaiah. If you recall, Isaiah was one of the prophets through whom God spoke long ago. His prophecy in Isaiah 53 is all about Christ's death—written nearly 700 years before He was born. The following is a stirring passage about Jesus and what He did for us.

Take your time and read through all of Isaiah 53. Then pray the Lord will kindle your love for Him afresh, as you draw near to the "blazing fire" of the cross today and your Savior who suffered there for you.

1. Before we look more closely at this passage, go back and reread Hebrews 1:2-13. Keep this picture of the glorious majesty and deity of Christ in mind as you study Isaiah. Think about the amazing contrast between Isaiah's description and this one in Hebrews.

2. Read Isaiah 53:2-3, 7-9. How does Isaiah describe Jesus, and how do people respond to Him?

3. Read Isaiah 53:4-6 (NLT) aloud and personalize it.
    Yet it was our weaknesses he carried;
    it was our sorrows that weighed him down.
    And we thought his troubles were a punishment from God,
    a punishment for his own sins!
    But he was pierced for our rebellion,
    crushed for our sins.

He was beaten so we could be whole.
He was whipped so we could be healed.
All of us, like sheep, have strayed away.
We have left God's paths to follow our own.
Yet the LORD *laid on him*
the sins of us all.

Now, stop and let these words sink into your soul.

4.   a. Where do you feel weak and powerless, what sorrows are you carrying today? You can draw near to Jesus and remember He carries your sorrows and pain (Psalm 55:22; Matthew 11:28-30).

   b. Is there something from your past or your present that keeps you from fully experiencing God's forgiveness? If so, write down whatever that is. Then, draw near to the "blazing fire" of the cross. Write out Isaiah 53:4-6 over the top of the sin and allow His forgiveness to wash over you.

Thank You, Lord Jesus, for being pierced through for my rebellion. I worship You for taking a brutal beating so that I can be whole and healed. Thank You for chasing after me even as I strayed—thank You for Your relentless pursuit. Thank You for dying for my sins and the sins of every person in my life, and of every person that has ever lived.

5.   a. Continue and read Isaiah 53:7-12.

b. Compare Isaiah 53:10-11 with Hebrews 9:11-14. Why was God pleased and satisfied with Christ's offering over any other sacrifice?

6.   What's the result of the "anguish of His soul" in verse 9:11-12, and why is this a picture of God's amazing grace?

Reflect & Respond

I just met with a student from Sri Lanka who was raised by her Buddhist mother and Muslim father. When she was in high school, the differences between the two religions became so confusing to her that she became an atheist. Then, through a series of events, she moved to the United States to attend a university in the Midwest, where her first roommate was a Christian. God was pursuing her. Soon she was invited to attend a dinner and Bible study for international students. She confessed that she went for the free dinner and not the Bible study. There, however, she first began to hear about Jesus. She told me she laughed at the notion Jesus was the Son of God who became a man. As she learned more about the cross, she also wondered, "Why wouldn't God save His Son from such a terrible death?"

As time went on, after learning more and attending church, she told her Bible study leader, "I think I'm falling in love with Jesus." Soon after, she placed her faith in Him, and today she's on the summer project I mentioned at the beginning of this lesson. She now faces overwhelming persecution as a result of her faith. As she sat and talked with me, I couldn't help but think of Jesus and Isaiah 53—He bears her sorrows and her grief. He is her great High Priest who was despised and forsaken of men, and He has made her whole.

ⓔ   If you're carrying unbearable grief or sorrow, draw near to Jesus. As Isaiah said, He bore our sins and also our sorrow and grief, and we press in close to the heart of our Savior.

"Let us then fearlessly and confidently and boldly draw near to the throne of grace (the throne of God's unmerited favor to us sinners), that we may receive mercy [for our failures] and find grace to help in good time for every need [appropriate help and well-timed help, coming just when we need it]" (Hebrews 4:16, AMP).

◎ If things are going well in your life—draw near to Jesus! Spend time at His feet and thank Him for His blessing. James 1:18 says, "Every good thing bestowed and every perfect gift comes from above, coming down from the Father of lights with whom there is no variation or shifting shadow." Share your joy with Christ, enjoy His goodness, and praise Him.

DAY FOUR

Retrace Your Steps

Another "gem" hidden among the details of Hebrews is the glorious fact that Jesus is God. Often I'll remind us to look again at Hebrews 1:1-3, but now that we're finished studying through Chapter 10, I think it's important to remember the majesty and sovereignty of God. He is the King and Lord of all. He gave Himself as the perfect sacrifice for our sin but never stopped being God.

We're going to look once again at these three verses, and with the help of the rest of the Bible, remind ourselves about whom we're studying. I've included the Amplified Translation, because its abundant use of words is a great example of how impossible it is to describe our awesome God and Savior.

Today we're going to read several passages aloud and praise Him. So, pray and ask the Spirit to rivet your attention on God. Pray He'll show you something fresh and new as you wonder at His excellence. Read the following passages aloud. Then stop to praise Him for a truth revealed or to talk to Him about something going on in your life, or simply meditate on what the passages say.

I've included some examples along the way.

1. **Deuteronomy 32:1-4**

    "Give ear, oh heavens, and let me speak;
    And let the earth hear the words of my mouth.
    Let my teaching drop as the rain,
    My speech distill as the dew,
    As the droplets on the fresh grass
    And as the showers on the herb.
    For I proclaim the name of the Lord;
    Ascribe greatness to our God!
    The Rock! His work is perfect,
    For all His ways are just;
    A God of faithfulness and without injustice,
    Righteous and upright is He."

Response: *I praise Your greatness, O God, that is evident in Your creation. I praise You for the perfect way You work in my life—even when I don't understand how or why. I praise You—You are my rock. You are stable and secure, You're my shelter in a storm; You are strong and powerful.*

2. **Hebrews 1:1-3**

"In many separate revelations [each of which set forth a portion of the Truth] and in different ways God spoke of old to [our] forefathers in and by the prophets, [But] in the last of these days He has spoken to us in [the person of a] Son, Whom He appointed Heir and lawful Owner of all things, also by and through Whom He created the worlds and the reaches of space and the ages of time [He made, produced, built, operated, and arranged them in order]. He is the sole expression of the glory of God [the Light-being, the out-raying or radiance of the divine], and He is the perfect imprint and very image of [God's] nature, upholding and maintaining and guiding and propelling the universe by His mighty word of power. When He had by offering Himself accomplished our cleansing of sins and riddance of guilt, He sat down at the right hand of the divine Majesty on high…." (AMP).

Response:

3. **Luke 4:18-19**

"The Spirit of the Lord is upon Me,
Because the He anointed Me to preach the Gospel to the poor,
He has sent Me to proclaim release to the captives, and recovery of sight to the blind;
To proclaim the favorable year of the Lord."

Response: *Thank You, Lord Jesus, for the woman who preached the Gospel to me when I was poor in spirit, lost and alone. Thank You for releasing me from my foolish ways, for protecting me, and forgiving my sins. Thank You for opening my eyes and allowing me to see You. Thank You for always being with me now when I'm poor in spirit and discouraged, when I can't find my way and I feel alone. Thank You that You never leave me and that nothing—absolutely nothing—can separate me from Your love.*

4. **John 14:10-14**

    "Do you not believe that I am in the Father, and the Father is in Me? The words that I say to you I do not speak on My own initiative, but the Father abiding in Me does His works. Believe Me that I am in the Father, and the Father in Me; otherwise believe on account of the works themselves. Truly, truly, I say to you, he who believes in Me, the works that I do shall he do also; and greater works that these shall he do; because I go to the Father. And whatever you ask in My name, that will I do, that the Father may be glorified in the Son. If you ask Me anything in My name, I will do it."

    Response:

5. **Psalm 145:1-7**

    "I will exalt you, my God the King;
    I will praise your name forever and ever.
    Every day I will praise you
    and extol your name forever and ever.
    Great is the Lord *and most worthy of praise;*
    his greatness no one can fathom.
    One generation will commend your works to another;
    they will tell of your mighty acts.
    They will speak of the glorious splendor of your majesty,
    and I will meditate on your wonderful works.
    They will tell of the power of your awesome works,
    and I will proclaim your great deeds.
    They will celebrate your abundant goodness
    and joyfully sing of your righteousness."

    Response:

Reflect & Respond

I'm often tempted to focus on ME rather than on the Lord, and it does my soul so much good to set my mind on Him and His greatness. I'm comforted by the fact that He's the creator of the universe, and nothing takes Him by surprise. I find that by focusing my attention on Him, I'm able to rest deep in my soul. Sometimes all it takes is reading some of these passages to remind me that He is so much bigger than my life, and He cares about the little things that trip me up.

◎ What has encouraged you the most about God throughout your time in the Word this week, and why?

◎ Pick up the phone and call someone in your family or your church, your neighborhood or your office, and talk to them about what you're learning about Jesus.

DAY FIVE

Hopefully this week's lesson has brought some clarity to the essential truths of the Christian life. I love going over these with old and new believers alike. It's always refreshing to look at Christ and the cross and remind ourselves of His amazing grace and unfathomable love. Go back over this teaching again and again until it's deeply ingrained in your heart. One of the most common reasons why believers begin to falter in their devotion to Christ is because they forget His love and forgiveness. I would encourage you to add some of the following to your list of memory verses:

I Peter 1:3-5

I John 1:9

Hebrews 7:25

Hebrews 13:5

In our next lesson, we're going to step into Hebrews 11—often called "The Great Hall of Faith." Enjoy this fifth day of your week and simply read Hebrews 11. If you need to catch up on some work, do so. Most of all, pray as you round the bend to the end of Hebrews. Ask Him to prepare you for the final three chapters. Pray that you'll not lose heart, but finish the study well.

---

1 C.J. Mahaney, *Living the Cross Centered Life*. (Colorado Springs: Multnomah Books, 2006), p. 13.
2 Ibid, p. 15.

The Rewards of Faith

Hebrews 11:1-40

My dreams, as a young girl, weren't very lofty. I had friends who aspired to be doctors and lawyers, politicians and journalists; I just wanted to get married. Even as a little girl, my sights were set on boys and being loved. I remember, as a skinny little 9-year-old, getting in deep trouble for calling boys on the phone. My mom lectured me—wagging her finger in my face, warning me of the danger of chasing after boys. I didn't really listen.

I had a major crush on David Wilmoth in second grade (as did most of the girls). On one occasion, in order to get his attention, I played "damsel in distress" with my friend Robin McAlpine and jumped off her balcony—twice—and broke my wrist. David never came. A year later, in an effort to snag David's affections, I begged him to play a game with me during recess. I pestered him to the point that he punched me in the stomach. Brutal—I know. But, I sort of deserved it. All through elementary school I wrote prayers in my diary to a God I didn't know, "Dear God, please give me a boyfriend."

My pursuit continued throughout junior high and high school. As I got older the stakes got higher—there was so much more to lose. I can laugh now about David Wilmoth and John Bailey, but the compromises I made in high school and college make me sad as I reflect back. My diary entries began to include a prayer to a God who seemed so far away, "Please forgive me for my sins." I remember many discussions with my dad about waiting for the right kind of guy—the guy who would willingly go to great lengths to see me and be with me. I'd shake my head in agreement, but inside I was afraid if I waited, I'd never find him. "Dear God, please give me a boyfriend."

I got to college and my longing persisted. I loved being in school, pledged a sorority, and even though I was in a long-distance relationship, I kept my options open—hoping that I'd finally find the right guy. In the background of my memories of my freshman year, Linda Ronstadt is singing, "I've been cheated, been mistreated, when will I find real love?" My long-distance boyfriend started talking about marriage that spring, so I decided to make it easy for him and quit school. I moved back home and waited for a proposal. Six months later we broke up. I vowed, at 19 years old, never to date again. Five months later, I was engaged to someone new.

My prayer was finally answered. I was planning a wedding with a shiny diamond on my finger. My dream was about to come true at last. I finally met a guy who really loved me, and I really loved him—and my dad liked him, too. Then, just 10 days before the ceremony, my fiancé dropped a bomb—over the phone. He didn't want to marry me, and the wedding was called off. I was devastated.

"I've been cheated, been mistreated, when will I find real love?"

In the midst of returning the wedding dress with the perfectly pleated skirt and the matching, shiny white shoes, relaying the terrible news to the guests on the rather long list, cancelling the flowers and the cake and the photographer, and piling up gifts that arrived daily in the mail, our neighbor, Lynn, invited me over for coffee. There was something different about her. She was religious, but in a compelling kind of way. She was fun to talk to and easy to be with and talked about God like she really knew Him. I knew she'd listen without offering me empty condolences. She did. After I'd shared the long, sordid story, Lynn explained the kind of love I was looking for wasn't found in a man (In my heart I was thinking, "I find that a little hard to believe."). The only place I'd find real love was in a relationship with Jesus Christ. Lynn shared John 3:16 (NASB) with me, "For God so loved the world that He gave His only begotten

Son, that whoever believes in Him will not perish but will have eternal life." She talked to me for a long time about God's love and forgiveness—both of which I desperately needed.

That sunny summer afternoon I went home, knelt down on the green shag carpet in my bedroom, and asked God to forgive my sins and asked Jesus to be my Savior. Heaven broke through and reached into my broken heart and saved me from the penalty and destruction of my sin, and He lavished me with His amazing grace. Because of God's great love and mercy, a new and eternal relationship was born along with a new and eternal purpose. Hopefully, at some point along the path, He broke into your heart and life, as well. He lavished you with His love and grace, and a new life of faith was born.

Hebrews 11 introduces us to a number of men and women who, thousands of years ago, encountered the God of the Universe, and their lives were changed, just like yours and mine. We'll learn about their faith, but even better, we'll learn about their God (and ours).

Lord, I pray that as we delve into Hebrews 11 that You'll use the lives of Noah, Abraham and Sarah, Moses and Joseph, and so many others to enliven our passion and desire to follow You by faith. Teach us what it means to walk by faith in such a way that we'll please You and experience Your reward.

DAY ONE

☐ Read Hebrews

Hebrews 11:1-19

Within days of receiving Christ and with Lynn's encouragement, I began praying to this God I barely knew. I moved to a new city and started life over. She told me to ask God for help to find a job and an apartment. I did. I soon found a job and moved into an apartment managed by a Christian—I could tell because he had a Bible on his desk. Jeff often talked to me about Jesus and going to church and joining a Bible study with other girls. I listened politely and continued to pursue boys, and as a result, I found myself in deeper trouble than I'd ever known. Yet, all the while I read the Bible Lynn gave me (even though it didn't make a lot of sense), and I talked often about my new relationship with Jesus.

My job as an administrative assistant paid the bills but promised little or no future. So, the Lord prompted my parents to convince me to return to college. Six months after packing my little red Honda and escaping home, I reluctantly returned. As I backed my car out of the parking lot, Jeff, who stood beside me during those trying months, said, "Get involved in Campus Crusade for Christ when you get on campus." This, for me, was a foundational step in this new life of faith.

God's invitation in my life began with a bang and a whisper. He heard my childhood prayers and stirred up a storm. He entered into my heart and transformed me instantly and ever so quietly. God invites each and every one of us to a life of faith—this invitation began in the very beginning with Abel and continues today thousands of years later. As we venture into Hebrews 11, we're going to look at God and faith and how the two go together. What's fascinating is the writer of Hebrews uses ordinary people, like you and me, to demonstrate faith and—most importantly of all—God's faithfulness.

As you begin your study today, reminisce about that moment in your life when Jesus reached into your heart and changed your life. Thank Him for relentlessly pursuing you then and now.

1.　a. Briefly describe how God initiated a relationship with you. Perhaps you received Christ when you were a small child; if so, be sure to include circumstances or conversations that caused you to continue to grow and walk with Christ.

Communicating Your Testimony
(provided by Campus Crusade for Christ, www.godsquad.com)

Your primary objective in writing and memorizing your testimony is to better relate to the average non-Christian. As you begin to work on it, consider what your life was like before you trusted Christ or you really began to see change.

Before I Accepted Christ (or gave Him complete control):
- What was my life like that will relate most to the non-Christian?
- What did my life revolve around? From what did I get my happiness or security? (Remember, the non-Christian is relying on something external to give him happiness and meaning.)
- How did those things let me down?

How I Received Christ (or gave Him complete control):
- When was the first time I heard the gospel? (Or when was I first exposed to dynamic Christianity?)
- What were my initial reactions?
- When did my attitude begin to change? Why?
- What were the doubts or struggles that went through my mind just before I accepted Christ?
- Why did I accept Christ?

After I Accepted Christ (or gave Him complete control):
- What are the specific changes Christ has made in my life?
- Are there any illustrations that would be helpful?
- Why am I motivated differently?

Helpful Hints:
- Write the way you speak-make the testimony yours.
- Choose a theme and carry it throughout the testimony.
- Don't be overly negative or positive. Be truthful.
- Don't criticize or name any church, denomination, organization, etc.
- Time limit should be 3 minutes. Practice it over and over until it becomes natural.

b. Reflect on the moment when you heard the Lord asking you to follow Christ. As you look back, how did you see the hand of God at work in your life through circumstances or people?

c. If you haven't responded to God's invitation to follow Him, explain why.

2. a. Read Hebrews 11:1 in the following two translations and describe faith:

"Now faith is the assurance of things hoped for, the conviction of things not seen" (Hebrews 11:1 NASB).

"Faith is the confidence that what we hope for will actually happen; it gives us assurance about things we cannot see" (Hebrews 11:1 NLT).

Remember, we learned in an earlier lesson that the hope of the Bible is something sure and certain, as opposed to the world's "hope," which is like a wish or desire.

b. How has your faith—assurance and conviction—grown over the course of your walk with Jesus?

3. I really enjoyed *March of the Penguins*, a movie that chronicled a year in the life of the Emperor Penguin. It was fascinating, to say the least. What I loved more than the amazing adventure of such strange creatures was the privilege of knowing the One who created them. I marvel at the creative handiwork of God.

a. According to Hebrews 11:3, what do we "understand by faith"?

b. How has creation helped you understand God?

4. As you read about some of the following men and women of faith, what did God ask each to do, and why did His request take faith, as defined in Hebrews 11:1? (Note: I've chosen just a few people to study in this week's lesson. But, I'd encourage you to take the time and look at every person this passage mentions. When you have the time, think about how God intervened in their lives and their examples of faith.)

Hebrews 11:7 (Genesis 5:32; 6:13-14; 7:1-6)

Hebrews 11:8-10 (Genesis 12:1-5)

Hebrews 11:11 (Genesis 18:12-14)

Hebrews 11:17-19 (Genesis 22:1-14)

5. As you noticed, God's warnings, His faithfulness, and His promises motivated these men and women to obedience. Notice also how often God asked them to step out in faith without knowing what was coming next. In addition, none of the men and women perfectly followed God and obeyed—Abraham and Sarah took circumstances into their own hands on a number of occasions; the only One who was consistently faithful was God. With this in mind, read Hebrews 11:6. How does this verse describe the faith that pleases God?

6. a. Read Hebrews 11:6 with Romans 4:18-22. What do you learn about the reality of Abraham's situation and the object of his faith in the Romans passage?

    b. How have you experienced God's faithfulness in the face of the impossible?

Reflect & Respond

Sometimes our temporal circumstances look bleak—like Abraham and Sarah's did. Genesis 16 details a moment in their lives when their faith wavered and they sidetracked. The result: Abraham fathered a child through Hagar, Sarah's maid. Sarah wasn't getting pregnant nor was she getting younger, so why not? Seemed like a viable solution, but it was a fleshly, human solution. How often we grow tired of waiting for God's provision or question His promise and decide to try things our way. No matter what we do, God always remains faithful and demonstrates amazing grace.

◎ Describe a time when you took things into your own hands rather than trusting God. What was the outcome, and what did you learn about God?

◎ Do you still feel guilty for your lack of faith? Based upon what you've learned from Hebrews, should you? Support your answer with Scripture.

I spent an evening with a young woman not long ago who desperately longs to get married. She had waited for a long time. She had grown impatient and fallen in love with a non-Christian. As they spent time together, she was unable to rest in the Lord, and eventually she ended the relationship. As she shared her story with me, she confessed, "Cas, I don't have faith to trust God with my future." I explained that God asks us to trust Him at this moment. He'll give us the faith we need to trust Him with the next hour.

@ What are you growing impatient about today?

@ What makes it difficult to trust God as you wait?

@ How can Noah, Abraham, or Sarah encourage you in your situation today?

DAY TWO

☐ Read Hebrews

Hebrews 11:23-27

Today we're going to spend our time looking into the life of Moses and the very beginning of Israel's journey. If you recall, Moses was mentioned earlier in Hebrews and is a beloved figure in Jewish history because God chose to use him, a human being made of flesh and bones, in a very significant way.

1. a. Read Hebrews 11:23 and record what you learn about Moses and his parents.

    b. Refer back and read Exodus 1:15-2:3 for more detail. Summarize Pharaoh's oppression and the faith of God's children.

    c. Describe what you learn about faith in both the Hebrews and Exodus passages.

2. Continue reading Exodus 2:4-10 and describe how God demonstrated His faithfulness through these circumstances.

3. Read Hebrews 11:24-27. What do you learn about Moses' character and choices?

4. Back in Genesis 18:14, God said to Abraham, "Is anything too difficult for the Lord?" Walk through Hebrews 11:7-29 and record all of the impossible things that happened.

Reflect & Respond

ⓔ In the lives of these men and women, God made the "humanly impossible" possible. In fact, most of His promises are fulfilled in very different ways from what we would expect. What have you learned about God in this lesson or throughout Hebrews that encourages you to trust Him? In particular, how does Moses' life motivate you to live by faith?

"And without faith it is impossible to please Him, for he who comes to God must believe that He is, and that He is a rewarder of those who seek Him" (Hebrews 11:6). This is another verse that I often repeat back to the Lord when I'm facing faith-stretching situations. What pleases God is a heart that seeks Him and an assurance and conviction that says, "Yes, I will trust You."

More often than not, God tests our faith through affliction (I Peter 1:6-8; James 1:2-4). You might long to have a husband or wife, children, good health, a strong family, a consistent job; God is saying, "Trust Me with this desire." Maybe you've been on a long road for a lot of years, waiting for an answer. Will you trust Him? Ponder this question—we'll come back to it again in Day Four.

DAY THREE

DIGGING DEEPER

What continues to amaze me as I study Hebrews is God's eternal plan. He used His servant Moses (like the covenant, the tabernacle, and the priesthood) as a shadow or copy of what is fulfilled in Christ in the New Testament. Moses, as he walked by faith, delivered the Israelites from physical bondage and slavery into a temporary rest. Jesus Christ delivered sinners from bondage and slavery to sin into a spiritual and eternal rest.

God is sovereign and in control of every point in history from before Moses to the present. He knows exactly what He's doing. These facts can bolster our confidence. We can trust God and His plan even when crazy things happen. And, when we're tempted to think chaos reigns rather than God or that our safety rests in Homeland Security instead of His all-powerful control, we can look back to His will and His ways and rest in His sovereignty by faith.

One of the benefits of growing older is the ability to look back at God's faithfulness over a long period of time. It's much easier to see His purpose and plan after several years have passed. For instance, I often thank God for protecting me from marrying the wrong man. At the time, I felt abandoned and unloved. Everything had crashed down around me, and I was lost, alone, and heart-broken. But now, several decades later, I can praise God for that broken engagement. As a result, I became a Christian, returned to college, and got involved in Campus Crusade for Christ, and I met and married Bob. I breathe a big sigh of relief every time I think about how things might have been.

Today we're going to spend some time looking at God's sovereign choice of us. He has a plan and purpose for your life and mine, just like He did for Noah, Abraham and Sarah, Moses, and all of the others. In addition, He is intimately involved in our lives.

It's to fun to experience Him and His presence as we go about the normal tasks of life. We can pray, and He provides a place to park and a good deal on new shoes. We can ask, and He gives us wisdom on what color to paint our house and creativity as we prepare a meal. He is involved in every part of our day. Enjoy that about the Lord, and thank Him for His provision and goodness.

Maybe you have a hard time believing God cares about you. It could be that your circumstances are so chaotic right now, you wonder whether or not God even is around. Perhaps tragedy has struck your family, and you're questioning God's goodness. Take a minute and lay your burden at His feet. Remember you can draw near to Him confidently—He's your Priest and King, and the Lover of your soul.

1.   a. Begin by reading and writing down Ephesians 1:3-5.

b. When did God chose you, and for what purpose did He predestine (to decide in advance) you?

c. Sit on that truth for a minute; let it sink into your heart and soul. Say it aloud and insert your name: *"He chose me (just like He chose Abraham and Sarah and Moses) in Him before the foundation of the world, and predestined me to adoption...."*

2. a. Look at Ephesians 2:10. For what purpose were you created in Christ Jesus, and when were those plans made? *"For we are God's masterpiece. He has created us anew in Christ Jesus, so we can do the good things he planned for us long ago."*

b. How does it make you feel to know (and begin to grasp) that you're God's masterpiece and that He mapped out a plan for your life before the world ever was?

c. What does faith have to do with accepting this truth?

3. a. Turn to Psalm 139 and read it all the way through.

    b. According to the following, what are some of the things God knows about you, and what are some of the things this teaches you about God?
   Psalm 139:1-5

      Psalm 139:7-10

      Psalm 139:13-18

c. Read Psalm 139:23-24. Why do you think the writer of the psalm ends with this response?

Reflect & Respond

◎ How will you respond to Psalm 139? Maybe you've been reminded that you can't escape the presence of the Lord—He hasn't abandoned you. Or, you've realized He has ordained all of your days, and He's involved in the best of days and the worst. Maybe you never realized that He has a plan for your life and promises to lead you. Write out a prayer and express your thoughts to Him.

There's something frighteningly wonderful about God knowing every breath we take, every word we utter (even before we do), and every aspect of our day. Like the psalmist says in verse six, "Such knowledge is too wonderful for me; it is too high I cannot attain to it." God is out of our league…and yet, He's intimately acquainted with all of our ways.

Remember: "Without faith it is impossible to please Him. For he who comes to God must believe that He is, and that He is a rewarder of those who seek Him" (Hebrews 11:6).

◎ How has your view of God expanded as a result of today's study, and what difference can that make in the rest of your week?

DAY FOUR

☐ Read Hebrews

Hebrews 11:29-40

Again, when I look back to those early years in my Christian life, I can clearly see God's hand in my life, guiding and protecting me. He brought believers along at "just the right time." At one particularly dark point in the first few months of my new faith, I was standing in line at the grocery store. I was so discouraged and depressed. I felt like I was going nowhere fast, and I was alone. Or so I thought. I glanced over to a book rounder. There sat a little book called, *The Jesus Person Promise Pocket Book.* Although my faith was brand new, I was confident that I was a "Jesus person" in desperate need of some promises. I bought that book and found such comfort as I read through verses promising peace, hope, protection, guidance. It was a picture of God's presence for me at a very tender point in my journey as a child of God.

I'm certain that you could tell stories about His hand in your life, as well—because He's just that way. He's intimately acquainted with all of our ways. He chose us, His masterpiece, for good works. He'll show us the way of faith.

The way of faith began thousands of years ago, and Hebrews 11:27-40 covers a multitude of faith-filled people who experienced a number of miraculous circumstances. We'll never plumb the depths of this passage of Hebrews. In fact, each time I read and look into this passage, I'm humbled. Pray today that you'll learn from the example of men and women who've gone before you—men and women "of whom the world was not worthy." They demonstrated faith—the assurance of things hoped for and the conviction of things not seen.

1. Read Hebrews 11:29-40 in the English Standard Version and underline the different ways faith was demonstrated.

    "By faith the people crossed the Red Sea as on dry land, but the Egyptians, when they attempted to do the same, were drowned. By faith the walls of Jericho fell down after they had been encircled for seven days. By faith Rahab the prostitute did not perish with those who were disobedient, because she had given a friendly welcome to the spies.

    And what more shall I say? For time would fail me to tell of Gideon, Barak, Samson, Jephthah, of David and Samuel and the prophets—who through faith conquered kingdoms, enforced justice, obtained promises, stopped the mouths of lions, quenched the power of fire, escaped the edge of the sword, were made strong out of weakness, became mighty in war, put foreign armies to flight. Women received back their dead by resurrection. Some were tortured, refusing to accept release, so that they might rise again to a better life. Others suffered mocking and flogging, and even chains and imprisonment. They were stoned, they were sawn in two, they were killed with the sword. They went about in skins of sheep and goats, destitute, afflicted, mistreated— of whom the world was not worthy—wandering about in deserts and mountains, and in dens and caves of the earth."

And all these, though commended through their faith, did not receive what was promised, since God had provided something better for us, that apart from us they should not be made perfect."

2. The writer of Hebrews doesn't give a lot of information regarding many of these circumstances or people. So, choose two or three of the following and read the Old Testament passages for a clearer picture. Write down how each demonstrated faith (keep in mind Hebrews 11:1, 6), and put yourself in their shoes while you're reading. Try to imagine what it would've been like to go through what they endured.

The children of Israel
   Hebrews 11:29/ Exodus 14:21-29

The Walls of Jericho
   Hebrews 11:30/ Joshua 6:15-20

Rahab
   Hebrews 11:31/Joshua 2:3-21

Gideon
   Hebrews 11:32/Judges 6-7

Daniel
   Hebrews 11:33/Daniel 6:1-24

A Widow
Hebrews 11:35/I Kings 17:17-24

b. What emotions did the people who you read about exhibit? If you were in their shoes, how would you have responded, and why?

3. a. What have you learned about faith from your study of Hebrews 11:29-40? How has your faith been strengthened?

b. God is still the God of the impossible. How have you seen Him take what seems impossible and make it work?

4. According to Hebrews 11:39, how did these people gain God's approval (keep Hebrews 11:1, 6 in mind)?

5.   Based upon all you've learned in Hebrews, what does it mean "they did not receive what was promised" (Hebrews 11:39), and why (Hebrews 11:40)? I've included commentator John MacArthur's thoughts to help.

"God has provided this 'something better' for us, that is for those under the New Covenant, which is why apart from us they should not be made perfect. That is, not until our time, the time of Christianity, could their salvation be completed, made perfect. Until Jesus' atoning work on the cross was accomplished, no salvation was complete, no matter how great the faith a believer may have had. Their salvation was based on what Christ would do; ours is based on what Christ has done. Their faith looked forward to promise; ours looks back to historical fact." [1]

Reflect & Respond

"And without faith it is impossible to please Him, for he who comes to God must believe that He is, and that He is a rewarder of those who seek Him" (Hebrews 11:6 NASB). This is another verse that I often repeat back to the Lord when I'm facing faith-stretching situations. What pleases God is a heart that seeks Him and an assurance and conviction that says, "Yes, I will trust You."

More often than not, God tests our faith through affliction (I Peter 1:6-8; James 1:2-4). You might long to have a husband or wife, children, good health, a strong family, a consistent job; God is saying, "Trust Me with this desire." Maybe you've been on a long road for a lot of years waiting for an answer, will you trust Him? Remember this from Day Two? You've had a chance to look at a lot of Scripture and a lot of real-life examples of faith and God's faithfulness. What have you been waiting for, and has this section of Hebrews encouraged you to trust the Lord? If so, how? If not, why?

Or, maybe something tragic has happened in your family. Recently my 17-year-old nephew committed suicide. I don't think I've walked through anything more difficult in my life—and I'm not his parent. In the face of the inexplicable, it's very difficult to walk by faith, to trust God's control, or His good plan and purpose. In fact, it all can sound trite in the face of heartrending situations. Yet, the Scripture we've looked at this week (and throughout our study) is absolutely true. God is really who He says He is. We can honestly lean on Him even in our darkest moments; He understands perfectly what it means to lose a child. He can handle our doubts or questions, our anger and pain.

@ Psalm 34 helps us understand how to praise and worship the Lord, how to find and experience joy in the midst of fear, trouble, and broken hearts. Read the entire Psalm out loud. Then, go back to the sections that speak to your heart and situation today. Insert your name or the names of others in your life. Praise the Lord for the ways that He enters into the difficulty of your life; ask Him, like the Psalmist does, to deliver you from your fears, to save you out of your troubles. Thank Him for being your Refuge and Provider, your Deliverer and Protector.

DAY FIVE

If you're caught up on all of your lessons and have time, I'd encourage you to look into the lives of everyone listed in Hebrews 11:32-38. It's quite amazing to read about their adventures in faith. I look forward to visiting with Rahab, the Shunnamite woman, Samuel, Daniel, and the others someday in heaven, and it's fun to have a small window into their lives now.

1. I've mentioned different promises that are in the Bible—some that remind us of the security of our salvation or God's forgiveness. I want to include a few today that have to do with God's trustworthiness in the face of the unknown and trying things of life.

   a. Compare the following with what you've learned from Hebrews 11:1,6 (NLT):
   Proverbs 3:5-6

   "Trust in the LORD with all your heart;
   do not depend on your own understanding.
   Seek his will in all you do,
   and he will show you which path to take."
   Ponder these two verses—no matter how familiar they might be.
   What do they tell you about God?
   What does it look like to depend on your own understanding?
   How do you "seek His will in all you do"?
   How do you know if you're on the right path?

   Romans 11:33-36

   "Oh, how great are God's riches and wisdom and knowledge! How impossible it
   is for us to understand his decisions and his ways!
   For who can know the LORD's thoughts?
   Who knows enough to give him advice?
   And who has given him so much
   that he needs to pay it back?
   For everything comes from him and exists by his power and is intended for his
   glory. All glory to him forever! Amen."

   b. These three verses from Romans have encouraged me almost more than any others as I've experienced the inexplicable. Read them carefully and thoughtfully.

   c. They're not pragmatic; they don't contain how-tos. So why might we find these encouraging?

For Further Study

- If your Bible has cross references (usually in the margin or at the bottom of the page), you'll find the Old Testament references for each. Take notes on what you learn about these people and their faith.

- I hope you've been working on memorizing different verses or passages in Hebrews. I'd encourage you to add Hebrews 11:1 and 6 to your list of verses.

1 MacArthur, *The MacArthur Bible Commentary Hebrews* (Chicago: Moody Bible Institute, 1983), page 369-370

Fix Your Eyes on Jesus

Hebrews 12:1-29

This week marks the beginning of another year of ministry for my colleagues and myself. As we gear up for the year ahead, we've been inundated with a variety of situations that tempt us to take our eyes off our mission and vision or to step out of the race all together. So, we gathered together as a group earlier this week to call upon His power and strength, to seek His wisdom, and to lay our burdens and decisions at His feet. We invited an older couple, friends of our ministry, who have served the Lord vigorously (and still do) for more than 55 years.

Before we began praying, this couple told us about a recent trip to Asia, where they heard story after story of God's faithfulness in the lives of believers in China, Taiwan, Thailand, and Hong Kong. They told us about visiting a South Korean church of more than 700,000 members. They described worshipping the Lord Jesus with 10,000 believers during one of the many Sunday gatherings. It refreshed us to hear about the faith of our Asian brothers and sisters that night. Some experience great and abundant fellowship, and others, because of their communist government, live under a constant threat of persecution. It was encouraging for us to hear about how our brothers and sisters in Asia trust the Lord in a variety of different ways.

That night we looked to Scripture to guide our prayer time. We turned to II Chronicles 20 and looked at King Jehoshaphat. War had been declared upon the nation of Israel, and Jehoshaphat was afraid. His immediate response was to pray. He gathered the whole nation together, and they "turned their attention to seek the Lord" (II Chronicles 20:3 NASB). He said, "O Lord, the God of our fathers, are You not God in the heavens? And are You not ruler over all the kingdoms of the nations? Power and might are in Your hand so that no one can stand against you" (II Chronicles 20:6 NASB). He went on to look back at God's faithfulness throughout Israel's history starting with Abraham, and then with great humility he said, "O our God, will You not judge them [Israel's enemies]? For we are powerless before this great multitude who are coming against us; nor do we know what to do, but our eyes are on You" (II Chronicles 20:12 NASB).

King Jehoshaphat, in the face of all-out war, immediately turned to God. He demonstrated faith by believing that God is: The God of our fathers, the God of heaven, the ruler over all kingdoms, the one who holds in His hand power and might. He, with the people, beseeched God to thwart their enemies and bring victory. We'll look at God's answer to their prayer later, but as I prayed with my friends the other night, I thought about believers in God who have gone before me, who walked by faith through incredible, strange, beautiful, frightening, and sorrowful situations. Their faith encourages me to stick it out; and God's faithfulness, power and might, goodness, justice, and supremacy humbles me and motivates me to pray and trust.

The Hebrew letter was written to believers, who in the face of persecution and discouragement, needed to endure: "Without faith it is impossible to please Him, for he who comes to God must believe that He is, and that He is a rewarder of those who seek Him" (Hebrews 11:6 NASB).

Throughout history men and women of God have endured and persevered in the face of great opposition. Their faith wasn't always perfect, but the object of their faith—our God and Savior—is perfect. "Therefore, since we have so great a cloud of witnesses surrounding us…let us run with endurance the race that is set before us, fixing our eyes on Jesus…" (Hebrews 12:1).

All of what we've studied and learned about the superiority of Jesus culminates in chapter 12 and 13. It's in these last two chapters that we apply chapters 1-11 to our own lives as we seek to endure and finish the marathon of life.

Today we're going to talk about Jesus, His discipline, and His Kingdom of grace. We've come a long way in our study of Hebrews, and we're almost finished. Pray the Lord will bring truths and principles together as you move into a more practical section of Hebrews. Pray your heart will be soft and ready to receive His Word. As you draw near to Jesus, pray that the reality of your relationship will strike home in a new way. Maybe you need fresh resolve to persevere to the end of our study—He will give you the endurance you need to finish well. I hope after rereading Hebrews several times, it makes more sense to you now than it did 11 weeks ago.

DAY ONE

☐ Read Hebrews

Hebrews 12:1-4;18-23

My study of Hebrews has included Tim Keller's sermons on Hebrews, which I've enjoyed and benefitted from greatly (They can be purchased at www.redeemer.com/store.). He often mentions that because of the persecution these believers endured, they were discouraged and downcast, and in need of "intense pastoral counseling." The writer of this letter knows their need. Remember in chapter 10, he remembers how they endured a "great conflict of suffering" and showed sympathy to prisoners. They joyfully accepted the seizure of their property and feared for their lives under Nero's reign. He is very aware of the complexities and questions that come with their circumstances and the hesitations that arise from their Jewish background. It is with all of this in mind that he likens the life of faith to a long-distance run (a metaphor used in other places in the New Testament), the final goal being "Mount Zion and the city of the living God, the heavenly Jerusalem" (Hebrews 12:22). In light of their reality, he does everything he can to point them to their Wonderful Counselor, Jesus Christ.

1. a. Define *persevere* or *endure* (whichever word your translation uses) at www.dictionary.com:

     b. Describe a time in your life when you learned the meaning of perseverance from an experience. Include things like the goal or outcome, what it felt like partway through, what it was like to have or not have encouragement from others, etc.

2. a. Read Hebrews 12:1-3, 18-24.

b. The main point in this passage is: Run the race with perseverance (Hebrews 12:1). For what purpose? (Use Scripture to support your answer.)

3. In order to "run the race with perseverance/endurance" we're told to lay aside encumbrances and sin, to fix our eyes on Jesus. We're going to explore each of these more in depth, but before we do, where are you in the race today? Are you weighed down, weary, and ready to lose heart? Have you lost your drive to persevere? Are you fully engaged and experiencing rest and joy in Jesus, or are you somewhere in the middle? Explain your answer.

4. "Let us strip off every weight that slows us down, especially the sin that so easily trips us up. And let us run with endurance the race God has set before us" (Hebrews 12:1 NLB). What things tend to keep you from cultivating your relationship with Jesus, things that take you slightly off course spiritually? Remember from our lesson on rest, it could even be good things, like being involved in several ministries in or outside of your church, or it might be your tendency to say "yes" to every opportunity that comes your way. It could be an unhealthy relationship or issues from your past that continually trip you up. Ask the Lord to shine His light (Ephesians 5:13) on the weights in your life.

5. a. The verse says to "lay aside especially the sin that so easily entangles us." What do you think is the difference between being "weighed down" and "entangled"?

b. Remember, if you know Jesus Christ as your Lord and Savior, all of your sin was bought and paid for at the cross. You're forgiven. But, you're still going to sin. It hinders your fellowship with God and often with other people. Again, ask the Lord to shine the light of His Word on anything that started out as a "weight" or an encumbrance and has turned into sin. It could be that you've allowed frustration with a co-worker to go unchecked, and it has turned into anger and resentment. Perhaps you've not forgiven someone for a wrong done to you in the past—you're either unwilling or you don't know how. Ask God's Holy Spirit to shine the light on and convict you of sin. Once He does, "call it sin (I John 1:9), call it forgiven, and call on God to change you."

6. "We do this (run the race with perseverance) by keeping (fixing NASB) our eyes on Jesus, the champion who initiates and perfects our faith. Because of the joy awaiting him, he endured the cross, disregarding its shame. Now he is seated in the place of honor beside God's throne" (Hebrews 12:2).

a. Why does the writer describe Jesus as our Champion (look back at Hebrews 2:9-10)?

b. Explain why Jesus is a great example of perseverance (use this and other Scripture to support your answer).

c. What did He focus on, and what was the end result of His endurance?

7. a. Based upon what we've studied today and throughout Hebrews, why keep/fix our eyes on Jesus?

    b. Do you think this helps? Why or why not?

I ask this because sometimes, before I determine to really look to Jesus, I wonder if it'll help. I'm tempted to think He can't be bothered with my little problems or that surely I'm strong enough to handle some of these tiny battles on my own. Recently, I was planning a meeting for the men and women who work on my ministry team. I wanted everyone to enjoy the time and feel like it was worth the effort. I'd planned well and had lots of food and coffee prepared, but for some reason I felt very nervous. As I prayed that morning the Holy Spirit reminded me, "Fix your eyes on Jesus, the author and perfecter of faith…." I smiled at the Lord, because just a few days before I'd written this lesson. So, I wrote my thoughts and feelings in my journal, cast my anxiety upon Him, and asked Him to help me keep my eyes on Him and not on me. It made a huge difference, in my soul, to take my eyes off of me and set them on Jesus.

Reflect & Respond

The words perseverance and endurance imply that this race is not a sprint but a marathon—it's a long distance race. Sometimes it's fun and relaxing, other times it's mundane, and at times—grueling. Consider Noah for a minute. He was commissioned to build an ark (even though there was no water) and to preach repentance and redemption to crowds of mockers and scoffers. It took him 100 years.

Abraham was called a "father of many nations." He was "as good as dead" and so was his wife's womb. Twenty-five years later his wife, who was in her 90s, gave birth to their first-born son, Isaac. Fast-forward to our Savior who emptied Himself and became a slave. He endured life on earth in a human body; He was despised and hated; He endured and persevered—for the joy set before Him—to the point of death on a cross.

@ When I really think about the plan of God from the beginning until the end, I understand why the writer of Hebrews was so intent upon everyone responding to the Gospel. Let me encourage you, if you have not yet placed your faith in Christ, to stop and consider what He did for you on the cross. Whatever is keeping you from surrendering your life to Him pales in comparison to the rich blessing of knowing and walking with Him.

@ The Christian life is an adventure, and sometimes it's exhilarating, often it's routine, and sometimes it's painful. When we fix our eyes on Jesus and lay aside encumbrances and sin, we're freed up to follow Him with greater focus and resolve.

I mentioned my nephew's suicide in a previous lesson. When I talk to my sister and her husband, they have enough faith to "take the next step." Sometimes fixing their eyes on Jesus means they need to talk about their son, the circumstances surrounding his death, or the funeral. Other times it's listening to a song of praise or sitting in a chair staring at the sky. It encourages me to watch the community of believers surround them and help them when they're too weary to lift their feet to take the next step. As I've walked through this with them, I've experienced a joy that flows from their sorrow, which is only possible because of Jesus.

Bob and I live next door to a retired couple who follow Christ. They're so encouraging to us. They know almost everybody in our complex because they listen, laugh, serve, and join in the lives of our neighbors. As a result, several have heard the Gospel and now attend church. Their joy in Christ is contagious, and even in their retirement, they continue to run the race with endurance.

@ What stage of the race are you in presently? How does this passage and Hebrews as a whole encourage you to persevere?

@ When we allow choices to weigh us down or entangle us, the race feels impossible. Sometimes laying aside sin seems impossible. If you're unsure how to experience freedom from encumbrances or sin, seek out someone at your church who walks with God and will point you to Jesus. He resisted sin to the point of shedding blood. He now lives in you, and His Spirit's power can set you free from whatever you're entangled in. There's joy in victory!

@ *Thank You, O Champion of my faith, for calling me out of my sin and into a relationship with You. Thank You for giving me the faith to believe in You and filling me with Your Spirit. You enable me to endure the race ahead. I confess my need for You, Your grace, and Your power every minute of every day. Remind me of Your presence, use others to point me to You. I cast off the weights (name them here if you have them). I confess my sin (name it here) and thank You for Your forgiveness. Fill me with Your Spirit's power and give me victory, O Lord.*

DAY TWO

☐ Read Hebrews

Hebrews 12:3-15

Did you notice that Hebrews 12:2 says that Jesus is the author and perfecter of faith? He gave us the faith we needed to believe, and He gives us the faith we need to persevere. Our job is to fix our eyes on Him and to consider or reflect upon what He endured, draw encouragement from His example, and find the ability to endure from His power. We'll dig into this more on Day Three. In the meantime, we're going to look at the example Jesus set and how that affects us as His children.

Psalm 119:129-131 says, "Your testimonies are wonderful; therefore my soul observes them. The unfolding of Your words give light; it gives understanding to the simple. I opened my mouth wide and panted, for I longed for Your [Word]."

"O Lord, unfold Your Word in my heart today and prepare me and help me learn. I'm simple-minded and unable to fully grasp Your truth. Thank You that I can understand because You give me Your wisdom and understanding. I'm here and ready to receive from You today Lord Jesus."

1. a. Read Hebrews 12 and get the context of the chapter in your mind.

   b. Compare Hebrews 12:3 with I Peter 2:18-23. According to each passage, what are we to gain from Christ's suffering and His example?

   c. Both of these passages bring to mind the great suffering that Jesus endured throughout His ministry on earth. The chances are good that we'll face similar hostility. What, according to both of these passages, is the benefit of looking to Jesus?

Peter, the disciple, reminds us that Christ "bore our sins in His body on the cross, so that we might die to sin and live to righteousness...." We learned in previous lessons that because of Christ's death, we've been set free from the penalty of sin. In addition, because of the cross and Christ's shed blood, we've been set free from the power of sin. We are now alive to righteousness because the Spirit lives in us. God is now our heavenly Father. He loves us, guides, and protects us, and He instructs and disciplines us.

Truth Search

2. Sometimes this discipline or instruction comes in the form of affliction, and other times, God reproves or rebukes us. Often His stern rebuke is the result of sin. Either way, Hebrews 12:6 says: "Those whom the Lord loves He disciplines, and He scourges every son whom He receives." In fact, if we don't receive discipline, we're considered "illegitimate children and not sons." The Father's discipline, in whatever form it comes, is the result and proof of His love and care. Read the following. What's the desired outcome of His discipline/instruction?

    Hebrews 12:7

    Hebrews 12:10

    Hebrews 12:11

3. Compare this passage with I Peter 1:6-9. Why is affliction necessary?

    I Peter 1:7

    I Peter 1:8

    I Peter 1:9

I remember reading these verses in I Peter for the first time when my mom was suffering from cancer. This passage encouraged me because I knew the Lord had a purpose for her suffering and mine, and I watched Him produce indescribable joy in my mom's life—despite the cancer. Just four months after her diagnosis—she died. Because of her faith in Jesus, my family and I rejoiced because we knew her suffering had ended and she stood in the presence of her Savior. The Lord continued to use this passage in my life long after her death. In the midst of sorrow and grief, the Lord ministered to my soul. He taught me about His sovereign control over all things (something I'd never thought about until my mom got sick). And, He taught me a little bit more about loving Him—even though I didn't see Him. He taught me a little more about faith and joy in the midst of a trial. It was a very instructive time in my life.

I've also experienced the Lord's "stern rebuke" in my life in many areas over the years. One that stands out, however, is my explosive anger. The Lord initially used His Word and other people to show me the deeper reasons for my anger early in my Christian life. I learned that my anger often surfaced when I felt a need for approval. I feared rejection, and rather than face that potential, I just got mad. I don't "blow" nearly as often as I used to, but when I do, I can almost always trace it back to feelings of insecurity. I continue to learn that I can take my fear, my insecurity, and my pride to His throne of grace and find mercy to help me.

4. In what areas of your life has God disciplined or instructed you, and what have you gained as a result?

5. Read Hebrews 12:14-17. What are we exhorted to do, and why do you think this particular instruction comes on the heels of Hebrews 12:5-11?

Hebrews 12:14

Hebrews 12:15

In Hebrews 12:15 the writer refers to Esau (Isaac's grandson) as an example of one who was immoral and godless. He cared more for momentary physical pleasure than he did about the future spiritual blessing that was his by right of birth. Remember that the writer of Hebrews often warns those in his audience who haven't responded seriously to Christ and His death on the cross.

6. We're reminded in Hebrews 12:15: "See to it that no one comes short of the grace of God."
    What do you think this means in light of the context of this chapter, and what does it mean in
    the context of your day to day life?

7. a. Where do you resist the Lord in your life most often?

    b. How will you respond to His instruction?

8. How can the transforming work He is doing in your life affect those around you—either at
    home, in school, or on the job?

Reflect & Respond

"Let us run with endurance the race that is set before us." As I write this study, the Summer Olympic Games are on television. Yesterday I watched the women's long-distance bike race. For nearly four hours, the women peddled against a torrential downpour. The slick roads and poor visibility made the already difficult journey even more arduous. But, their training paid off, and everyone persevered through the weather, the uphill climbs, and finished the long race. The gold-medal winner crossed the finish line wearing a huge smile. Despite her exhaustion she was filled with joy—she finished the race and won the prize.

The race before us is not easy. Conditions are unpredictable, and we don't know what's ahead. But, one thing we do know is the One who set the course: Jesus, the author and perfecter of our faith. He uses the steep terrain and the grueling conditions to train us to endure. He trains us to fix our eyes on Him and the eternal reward. He uses the routine of life, along with pain and suffering, to point us and others to Him.

Joseph Stowell, in his book *Following Christ,* writes, "How do we trigger His transforming work in us? This happens in several ways. We must recognize that He acts on the point of change that is most strategic. Not surprisingly, this will often be the point of our greatest resistance. If we are living by our passions, he will challenge our flirtations and sexual addictions. If we harbor bitterness, He will call us to discard that long-standing grudge that has seemingly protected us, expressed our rage, and satisfied our sense of hurt. If we are addicted to our glory and gain in the workplace, He will require a new perspective that transforms our job from a place of self-serving to a platform for advancing His kingdom." [1]

DAY THREE

☐ Read Hebrews

Digging Deeper

My husband Bob and I spent five weeks earlier this summer in Siena, Italy with nine college students and two Campus Crusade for Christ staff. Our team of 13 spent time at the University of Siena telling Italian students about Jesus. Around 95 percent of the Italian population says their Catholic while only two percent attend church regularly. It was fascinating to talk with young men and women about God, the Bible, and Jesus Christ. Several times, as I shared my personal story and the Gospel, students would say, "I've never heard of a love like this before." Their intriguing response reminded me in a fresh way that I actually enjoy a *relationship* with God. It's vital and growing, it ebbs and flows, it's confusing and endearing, and it's going on right now and for eternity. Moreover, God dropped Bob and me and our team in Italy for the express purpose of telling particular students about Him because He is pursuing a relationship with them. Near the end of our trip, my friend Megan and I shared the gospel with two freshman girls, Giulia and Irene, who placed their faith in Christ. I continue to pray for them and their new relationship with Him, and even though they don't really understand exactly what happened that day in Siena, I pray that they'll learn to run the race with endurance. Even more, I pray they'll learn to fix their eyes on Jesus—the author and perfecter of their faith.

As we've learned in this week's lesson, the Lord is actively involved in our growth and maturity. He allows all sorts of things along the course of our race to push us and point us to Him. Like Giulia and Irene, I began to walk with Christ when I was in college. I was desperate on many levels, and Jesus made Himself very real and obvious to me. As I matured, I began to pray and then listen to the Lord. I started to read my Bible and seek His face. Other believers came into my life and taught me about the Holy Spirit's presence and power in my life. Over time, I began to take the things I learned and impart them to others, which meant I needed to spend even more time in the Word and study.

The Lord used, among other things, marriage, friendships, working relationships, money and the lack thereof, places to live, infertility, moving from one state to another and then overseas, health problems, travel, a dog, family, a garden, the ocean, and my dad to teach me what it means to "fix my eyes on Jesus." There's not a neat and tidy formula to this life of faith, but there is a living and loving Savior who delights in having a relationship with you and me.

Today we're going to spend some time pondering what it means to fix our eyes on Jesus. I'll share with you some thoughts and ideas that have helped me over the years. I'm very much in process, still learning and wondering what it means to love Jesus with a whole heart, unencumbered by the "stuff of life." So, pray with me that the Lord will use this day to help us become more dependent upon Him.

The peril of writing a Bible study is learning firsthand the truths I'm teaching. After several days of wrestling through this week's lesson, I finally finished. I went to close the document on my computer and rather than saving it, I deleted it. Hours worth of work gone in an instant. I sat motionless for a few minutes and then went for a walk. I felt frustrated and discouraged. As I talked to the Lord, He reminded me to fix my eyes on Jesus, rest in Him, and show Him gratitude. So, by faith I did, and here I am again.

1.　a. The race we're running is daily and so is the call to fix our eyes on Jesus. What happened in your life this week that frustrated, confused, irritated, or perplexed you? It might be something as simple as forgetting bananas at the grocery store, losing a receipt, or running behind in your laundry.

　　b. How did Jesus comfort or meet you in that moment? Or explain why you chose not to bring Him into that moment.

　　c. If someone were to ask you, "What does it mean to 'fix my eyes on Jesus?'", what would you say?

2.　Hebrews 12 surfaced a rather routine area of life, and that's relationships. Hebrews 12:14 says, "Pursue peace with all men, and the sanctification without which no one will see the Lord." A parallel verse is found in Romans 12:18, "If possible, so far as it depends upon you, be at peace with all men."

　a. What do you think these two verses mean?

b. Now, look at Ephesians 4:1-3. What are some key ingredients in peaceful relationships?

3. Compare these with Philippians 2:1-8. Jesus is our ultimate example in humble, selfless, and ultimately peaceful relationships. With this passage in mind, what does it look like to "fix our eyes on Jesus" in the midst of relating with others?

4. Hebrews 12:14 also addresses the issue of bitterness. All kinds of things can produce bitterness, animosity, resentment, or hostility. Probably the most common reason for bitterness, however, is a lack of forgiveness. An unforgiving heart can certainly weigh us down and impede our spiritual progress. The road to forgiveness comes by first grasping what Jesus did for you and me at the cross.

    Muriel Cook in her book, *Kitchen Table Counseling*, writes, "Forgiveness is an act of the will; healing is the process. God's Word tells us to love our enemies and pray for our persecutors (see Matthew 5:44). We're told to feed them (see Romans 12:20) and to love one another (see I John 4:7). But nowhere in the bible does it say to do these things if we feel like it. It simply tells us to do them. Why? Because if we wait until we feel like it, we'll never do them. We don't always want to forgive, but Christ in us always does [sic]. We have to choose to forgive with our will." [2]

    a. Read Matthew 18:21-27. What did the king do for the slave who owed him more than 10,000,000 in silver, and why (keep your eyes on the text)?

b. According to Matthew 18:28-30, how did the slave, who was forgiven a HUGE debt, respond to his fellow slave, and why?

c. What did the king do according to Matthew 18:31-35, and why?

d. What does this story teach about the Gospel and forgiveness?

Reflect & Respond

Jesus hasn't left us to run the race on our own. He's given us a Helper—the Holy Spirit, who lives in the heart of every believer. You'll recall several lessons back we looked at God's Holy Spirit. We learned He's our guide and teacher, and He lives in us, and we're His temple. This truth is really quite amazing. The God of the Universe, the Creator of it all, lives in you and me. We have everything we need pertaining to life and godliness (II Peter 1:2). In order to experience God's indwelling power, we need to surrender our will to His.

@ If you've been harboring bitterness toward someone, ask the Lord to help you to understand His forgiveness in such a way that you can show mercy and forgive. Healing from possible wounds will come, but it begins with forgiveness.

@ Look closely at Philippians 2:12-13. How is what feels impossible (like doing "nothing from selfishness or empty conceit"; being at peace with all men; forgiveness) possible?

DAY FOUR

☐ Read Hebrews Read Hebrews

Hebrews 12:18-29

We're nearing the end of Hebrews, and I imagine the writer, who is passionate about his love for Jesus, also cares deeply about those to whom he's writing. He has taken great pains to lift and exalt Jesus high above mere copies and shadows of earthly things and to make sure that his readers understand the holiness and grace of God. As we near the end of chapter 12, he issues another strong warning to anyone who has yet to accept the incredible gift of God in Christ.

1. Read Hebrews 12:18-29.

2. As is true for the whole of Hebrews, this passage compares the Old Covenant with the New.

   a. Look back to Exodus 19:9-18 along with Hebrews 12:18-21, and write down what you observe about Mount Sinai and the people's response.

   b. Why do you think Moses and the children of Israel were so afraid?

3. According to Hebrews 12:22-24, what's the difference between Mount Sinai and Mount Zion, and why?

4. In Hebrews 11:13-16, those who lived as aliens, strangers, and exiles on the earth considered themselves citizens of a heavenly city, which the writer describes in Hebrews 12:22-24. All of us are citizens of heaven who live as aliens on earth. Jesus, while on earth, boggled the minds of those who listened. His instruction for life was very different than what they'd taught and heard.

a. How does Jesus tell us to live, and why does this set us apart?
Matthew 5:14-15

Matthew 5:44-48

Matthew 7:1-5

b. Look at the following and write down what you discover about the purpose behind this lifestyle:
I Peter 2:9-10

Matthew 5:16

In an earlier lesson, I mentioned my neighbors who are well known by most of the people in our neighborhood. I've watched them befriend a woman who is going through a divorce. Her husband left after 16 years of marriage because he didn't love her anymore. Then, someone stole her checkbook and all of the money in her account. My neighbors entered into her life, loved and listened to her, and invited her to church and over for dinner, and they've shared the love of Jesus with her. They've explained that Jesus can bear her burdens and help her through this difficult time. These neighbors live out the Gospel and let their light shine.

5. Hebrews 12:25-26 and Hebrews 10:26-31 issue a strong warning for those who refuse Him. What is the warning?

"The true God is not tame, nor does he spoil his children. He is like a fire: the holiness of God, emphasized through the Temple ritual, is not undermined by the fact that, in the new covenant, his people are invited into his presence in a new way…. It isn't that God has stopped being holy. God hasn't changed a bit. It is, rather, that Jesus has opened a new and living path, through the 'curtain' and right up to him. Only when we remind ourselves of God's holiness do we fully appreciate the significance of what Jesus achieved. It is noticeable that, where thinkers have spoken of God without stressing his all-consuming holiness, the meaning of the cross is downgraded in proportion…. The appropriate response, therefore, is gratitude and worship." [3]

6. a. Look at II Peter 3:10-13. These three verses enhance our understanding of the promise in Hebrews 12:26. Write down the promise and your observations of what's ahead.

b. Read II Peter 3:9. What do you learn about God?

The heavens and the earth, as we know it today, will pass away. The end is near and so is a brand-new beginning. God calls all of us, as aliens and strangers, to proclaim His excellencies. You and I have a sure and steadfast hope, a salvation that's secure, and a Savior who is God. He is patiently waiting for all to come to repentance. I'm so thankful for this truth.

Reflect & Respond

Our future is unshakable; heaven is a real place; and God in all of His glory will reign victorious. Our response? Let's show Him gratitude and offer acceptable service with reverence and awe. One of my prayers as I write is that we will lift our eyes up to our glorious Savior. It's so easy sometimes to concentrate on what we need to "do" for Him. Let us rest in the gift of relationship with Him. Let us enjoy our Savior who is alive, glorious, and awesome.

Tonight as I lamented the loss of my hard work, I gazed up into the night sky and thanked God for the stars and the moon, the sweet smell of summer nights, my home, and my husband.

◎ What about you, what are you thankful for? Show Him gratitude by taking time to notice His handiwork, His answer to prayer, His wisdom, and His work in your heart as you study His Word. Thank Him that you can serve Him with reverence and awe as you bus tables or change the oil or your child's diapers.

◎ Rejoice that you come to Mount Zion, and the city of the living God where Jesus sits on the throne.

DAY FIVE

☐ Read Hebrews Read Hebrews

We covered a lot of intense truth in this week's lesson. Let me reiterate that my desire for us as we study Hebrews isn't to plow through the chapters, which is tempting at times, but to ponder the truths of God's Word and to listen closely to the Spirit's voice as we consider Jesus.

1. So, go back through each day's section, and pray for wisdom and clarity from the Lord. Is He touching on an area of perseverance right now? Is there sin or an encumbrance that He has highlighted that you need to ponder more?

2. I think it might be easy to whiz by bitterness and forgiveness because both often surface painful areas in our lives. Let me encourage you to go back. Be sure that you're allowing time for the Spirit to guide you in this area.

3. And, there's wonder and awe in the subject of heaven and the future kingdom. It's hard to imagine how Adam and Eve, Noah, Abraham, Sarah, Joseph, or Moses could know much about this "better country" because we don't know too much either. But, what we do know is fascinating and so hopeful. Perhaps you need to camp for awhile in the heavens and think about the city of God that's to come. Go back to the passages listed in this week's lesson, and read them again. Meditate on what they say, and by faith, praise God for the hope that you have in Jesus both now and in the future.

For Further Study

God's love is an attribute that is most comforting and yet, incomprehensible. His love, which it's perfect, is hard to grasp, because all we have to compare it with is the love we experience from other people. Human love is fickle and conditional while God's love is unchanging and unconditional; and, His love is rooted in all of who He is. I think it takes a lifetime to scratch the surface of understanding His love.

- Look up the following verses and passages, and write down what you discover about God's love.

    Psalm 117:2

    John 3:16

    Ephesians 3:16-18

    I John 4:18-19

- What do you learn about God's love that is different about anyone else's?

- How does God's perfect love encourage you in your circumstances today?

1 Joseph Stowell, *Following Christ* (Zondervan, Grand Rapids, 1996) p. 101.

2 Muriel Cook, *Kitchen Table Counseling* (Colorado Springs, NavPress, 2006) pp. 47-48.

3 Tom Wright, *Hebrews for Everyone.* (Perthshire: Ashford Colour Press, 2004). page 166

Live Your Life for Jesus

Hebrews 13:1-25

I hope that you've enjoyed studying Hebrews as much as I have. Something that strikes me is God's plan is huge, He is absolutely in control, and Jesus Christ is more amazing and awesome than I could ever imagine. I recently read this quote in a book on the plan of redemption, and I think it describes what we've seen in our brief look at Hebrews. "God's grace seen in his dealings with Israel is part of a living process which comes to its climax in his work of grace, the gospel, that is in the historical events of the Christ who is Jesus of Nazareth." [1] For twelve weeks we've observed and studied this "living process" laid out for us in Hebrews. We lifted our eyes up to see Jesus, our King and Savior, right from the beginning. We touched on Jesus' superiority to angels, His victory over sin and death, and learned that Moses, though a significant figure in Israel's history, was God's servant while Jesus is God's Son. We grappled with our promised rest, our vulnerability before God and His Word, and found mercy at the feet of our Great High Priest and His throne of grace. Then we were introduced to Melchizedek, but not without a plea to press on to maturity. We learned that, like Melchizedek, Jesus is both Priest and King. Then we honed in on the main point: "We have such a high priest, who has taken his seat at the right hand of the throne of the Majesty in the heavens, a minister in the sanctuary, and in the true tabernacle, which the Lord pitched, not man" (Hebrews 8:1-2). Jesus Christ, by offering Himself as the perfect sacrifice for sin, made it possible for us to enter into the Most Holy Place. Therefore, we can draw near to God with full confidence because of Jesus our sure and steadfast hope, the anchor of our soul. Wow, what a Savior!

These chapters weren't without stern warning. We learned the community of believers (recipients of this letter) included people who had yet to take Jesus Christ seriously. The writer weaves the seriousness of salvation throughout all 12 chapters.

We then took a walk through the annals of Biblical history and observed how faith pleases God, how He used Abel and Enoch, Noah, Abraham and Sarah, Joseph and Moses, and so many others in His plan of redemption—culminating in the death, burial, and resurrection of Jesus. These men and women died without receiving the promises, but while they lived, they looked forward to a Savior and the city of God—all by faith.

Our study culminated at Mount Zion, the city of the living God, the new Jerusalem, where Jesus Christ reigns as King and Lord over all. And as we close, we learn the "living process" of redemption continues until that day, and we urged to take an active part in this race of endurance. The key to finishing well: "Fix our eyes on Jesus."

As we wrap up our study of Hebrews, pray the Lord will help you to not simply persevere and finish but to finish well. Ask Him to give you ears to hear His voice of truth.

DAY ONE

☐ Read Hebrews

Hebrews 13:1-8

Jesus commissioned us to "Go and make disciples of all nations...." (Matthew 28:19), and at the University of Siena this summer, my team and I had numerous opportunities to share the Gospel with students from all over the world: Israel, Romania, Albania, Togo, the Dominican Republic, Great Britain, Palestine, and Ireland, to name a few. One day while on a walk, I was struck not only by the fact that the Lord placed us in Italy to talk with students about the love and forgiveness of Jesus, but also He allowed our paths to cross with a variety of tribes, tongues, and nations who will inhabit the heavenly city.

1. When heaven's inhabitants stand together to worship and praise the King, I think it will look like a brightly colored tapestry. Look up the following verses, and record what more you discover about the citizens in God's heavenly city.

    Revelation 5:9

    Revelation 7:9-10

    Revelation 15:3-4

The kingdom of heaven is coming—in Lesson 11 we looked at what's promised in Hebrews 12:27-28 and II Peter 3:9-13. It's also important to remember as children of God we represent the kingdom of heaven right now. Remember, we're aliens and strangers, exiles on earth. The Lord has us here for a variety of reasons, one of which is to live out the Gospel—love, forgiveness, hope, security, and rest—among those who don't know Christ. Hebrews 13:1-17 picks up where the writer's practical instruction left off in Hebrews 12:17.

2. We're advised in Hebrews 13:1-8 to do several things. Read Hebrews 13:2-6 and answer the following questions:

    a. What are we advised to do?
       Hebrews 13:1

       Hebrews 13:2

       Hebrews 13:3

       Hebrews 13:4

       Hebrews 13:5a

       Hebrews 13:7

    b. Think about the world you live in—taking kids to school and soccer or working at a coffee shop, engineering firm, retirement home, or university. Why, in light of your experience and observations, do you think the writer highlights these particular actions and attitudes? (comment on one or two)

It's tempting to look at this list and shine the spotlight on our ability to walk with the Lord and wonder, "How am I ever going to remember all of this? What if I fail?" or "I'm going to do everything I can to live for Jesus no matter what." Jonathon Edwards, a fiery Puritan preacher, once wrote, *"It was my continual strife day and night, and constant inquiry, how I should be more holy, and live more holily, and more becoming a child of God, and disciple of Christ. I sought an increase of grace and holiness, and that I might live an holy life, with vastly more earnestness, that ever I sought grace, before I had it. I used to be continually examining myself, and studying and contriving for likely ways and means, how I should live holily, with far greater diligence and earnestness….My experience had not then taught me, as it has done since, my extreme feebleness and impotence."* [2]

3. There's no getting around the fact we need Jesus Christ. We are feeble and prone to sin and failure. It's for this very reason the Lord indwells us with the Helper, His Holy Spirit. Every day we need to remember the Lord Jesus is at the center of it all and fix our eyes on Him.

    a. Look at the following. What does the writer include about Jesus in this section of Hebrews?
    Hebrews 13:5b

    Hebrews 13:6

    Hebrews 13:8

    b. What about these specific truths comfort you, and why?

Reflect & Respond

Maybe you need His help to love someone in particular; perhaps your life is too busy to show hospitality to anyone, let alone a stranger. In the day when this letter was written, believers were imprisoned for their faith, and the same is true today. Are you aware of and do you pray for the persecuted church?

It could be you're compromising your marriage through a relationship at work, pornography, movies, or books. We all face fleshly temptations, such as self-centeredness, discontentment, bitterness, sex, and money. In His grace, He convicts, instructs, and disciplines us. If we listen to His voice, recognize and admit our desperate need, and yield to His power and will, we are able to overcome even the strongest enticements.

In my experience, thoughts or temptations sometimes come in and out of my mind, and if they are nipped in the bud, they don't become encumbrances or sin. I've been working on acknowledging those thoughts, my inadequacies, my discontentment or want for more and putting whatever it might be at Jesus' feet. Sometimes it's a quick, "Help me love this person in my life today." Or I'll ask Him to help me remember to pray for the persecuted church. Other times, I'll talk with the Lord about why certain things are on my mind. He often shows me I'm spending too much time at the mall or in front of the television. Sometimes He reveals that the source of my fear is my desire to please people instead of Him (Galatians 1:10). Communing with Him, intimately, means talking with Him about everything; often a good, long conversation with the Lord with the Bible open helps more than anything.

ⓔ What about you? Are you taking the time to sit and talk to Jesus? Psalm 62:8 says, "Trust in Him at all times, pour out your heart before Him; God is a refuge for us." He will never leave you or forsake you. With confidence you can say, "He is my helper, I will not be afraid, what can man do to me?"

Make a list of the things that are true of Jesus that mean a lot to you at this point in your life (Reflect back over your study of Hebrews.). Over the top of your list write, "Jesus Christ is the same yesterday and today, yes and forever."

ⓔ I take great comfort in the fact the Lord doesn't change—ever. Micah 7:18-20 is like a beautiful love song. Finish your time with the Lord today by reading and writing down this "song." Listen closely, you might hear Him singing it to you.

DAY TWO

☐ Read Hebrews

Hebrews 13:9-17

Jesus Christ's superior sacrifice was highlighted throughout so much of Hebrews, and understandably so. His perfect sacrifice made it possible for us to have a relationship with Him, and no one person deserved this gift. He willingly suffered and died out of obedience to His Father for us. This group of Jewish believers needed this instruction. They were tempted to revert back to the old sacrificial system and old rituals. The writer takes one last opportunity to highlight Jesus Christ as the Superior Sacrifice. The Old Covenant is obsolete. We are now invited to join Jesus "outside the camp."

We're nearing the end of our study, so for the sake of review, use verses in Hebrews to support your answers for today's questions.

1. a. Read Hebrews 13:9-17 from the New Living Translation:

   So do not be attracted by strange, new ideas. Your strength comes from God's grace, not from rules about food, which don't help those who follow them.

   We have an altar from which the priests in the Tabernacle have no right to eat. Under the old system, the high priest brought the blood of animals into the Holy Place as a sacrifice for sin, and the bodies of the animals were burned outside the camp. So also Jesus suffered and died outside the city gates to make his people holy by means of his own blood. So let us go out to him, outside the camp, and bear the disgrace he bore. For this world is not our permanent home; we are looking forward to a home yet to come.

   Therefore, let us offer through Jesus a continual sacrifice of praise to God, proclaiming our allegiance to his name. And don't forget to do good and to share with those in need. These are the sacrifices that please God.

   Obey your spiritual leaders, and do what they say. Their work is to watch over your souls, and they are accountable to God. Give them reason to do this with joy and not with sorrow. That would certainly not be for your benefit.

   b. According to Hebrews 13:9 what are we to avoid?

c. What does "your strength comes from God's grace" mean?

2.   a. Hebrews 13:10-13 contrasts the difference between the earthly altar and the heavenly one (Jesus Christ); and the early city with the heavenly one. Why is it significant that Jesus suffered outside the city?

b. Why does the writer remind us that our permanent home is yet to come?

The phrase, "So let us go out to him, outside the camp, and bear the disgrace he bore" (Hebrews 13:13) has specific and significant meaning to this Jewish audience. H.A. Ironside (He wrote many commentaries in his day that make the Bible easy to understand.) helped me with this,

"'Jesus also, that He might sanctify the people with His own blood,' that is, that He might set them apart to God in all the value of His atoning work, 'suffered without the gate.' He took the outside place there to bear the judgment that our sins deserved, and now we put our trust in Him, the rejected One, as our Saviour, and confess Him as our Lord.... To these Hebrews this would mean even more than to believers in a later day, who have never been attached as they were to a divinely ordained system which was afterwards disowned by God. The deepest affections of their hearts, until they knew Christ, were twined about that system.... It meant the breaking of the tenderest of ties, and would necessarily lead to the gravest misunderstandings, but in no other way could they be faithful to the One whom the nation of the Jews had refused, but who had bought them with His blood." [3]

3.   There are implications for us today when we choose to live "outside the camp" of the world's system, when we choose to follow Jesus Christ rather than the ways of the world. How have you experienced misunderstanding or ridicule because of your faith in Him?

4.   Often, when I share the Gospel with people who go to church regularly, they don't recognize their need for a Savior. They believe they can earn their way to God. Based upon what you've learned from Hebrews and the Jewish system, how would you explain the Gospel? Include three or four main points, and explain your choice. Remember, to aid in your review, use only verses from Hebrews.

Truth Search

Dictionary.com defines *sacrifice* as "the surrender or destruction of something prized or desirable for the sake of something considered as having a higher or more pressing claim."

5.   a. The Lord isn't looking for atoning sacrifices any longer. According to Hebrews 13:14-17, what kind of sacrifices please Him?

b. Why do you think these three things are considered sacrifices?

c. Compare these verses with the following. What more do you learn about pleasing sacrifices? Psalm 51:15-17

Micah 6:6-8

Romans 12:1-2

Reflect & Respond

Hebrews 13:7 says, "Remember those who led you, who spoke the word of God to you; and considering the outcome of their way of life, imitate their faith." In an earlier lesson, I mentioned my friend Dorothy. She was a great example of someone who offered the Lord sacrifices of praise. The fruit of her lips truly did give thanks to His name. Another man who had great influence in my life, Bud Hinkson (a pioneer in Campus Ministry with Campus Crusade for Christ), was one of the most thankful men I've ever met. He died many years ago, but I still remember how thankfulness and joy dripped from his lips. It's not always easy to thank and praise the Lord. Yet, it's an expression of trust. We can choose to say, "Lord, I don't feel thankful right now, but I trust You're sovereign. You are my helper, and You never change."

© Reflect back over your life. Who has led you spiritually? Describe this person's impact on your life.

© If this person is still alive, write him/her a note to express your thankfulness. If not, spend some time thanking the Lord for using him/her in your life.

DAY THREE

☐ Read Hebrews

Review

Over the past 12 weeks or so, you've spent a lot of time studying, reading, and pondering the book of Hebrews. With your Bible closed, walk through all 13 chapters and see what you've learned.

1. First, what do you remember about each chapter?

    1: God, angels

    2:

    3:

    4:

    5:

    6:

    7:

    8:

9:

10:

11:

12:

13:

2. Without looking, what is the main idea of Hebrews?

3. Over the years, I've memorized a few verses from each chapter of a book I study. It helps me remember what I studied. Here are the verses I've chosen to help me remember the Gospel and gift of Jesus, and they compel me to press on. Some of these I already have memorized, and some I'm going to memorize now.

    Look at these and write down the main idea of each.
    Hebrews 1-6

    Hebrews 1:1-3

Hebrews 2:9, 14-15, 18

Hebrews 3:1, 6

Hebrews 4:10-13

Hebrews 4:14-16

Hebrews 5:7-9

Hebrews 6:11

Hebrews 7-13

Hebrews 7:25

Hebrews 8:1-2

Hebrews 9:11-14

Hebrews 10:19-25

Hebrews 11:1,6

Hebrews 12:1-3

Hebrews 12:14-16

Hebrews 13:5-8

Reflect & Respond

◎ How has the Lord used this study to change your life? Maybe your perspective of Jesus has changed, or your attitude toward Him has been refreshed, or you've laid aside a particular sin. Ask Him to help you remember things He has taught you and write them here.

◎ Write out a prayer of thanksgiving to the Lord.

DAY FOUR

☐ Read Hebrews

Hebrews 13:18-25

Like many Epistles in the New Testament, Hebrews ends with a few personal thoughts and a benediction. Down through the ages students have looked for clues of authorship within these personal details. We can speculate, but I don't think we'll know until heaven who wrote this great letter. We do learn a few things about him and his heart in these last few verses.

1. a. Read Hebrews 13:18-19, 22-25. What you learn about the personal side of the author and his friends?

    b. Look at Hebrews 13:23. What fact adds importance and meaning to Hebrews 13:2?

2. a. I love the benediction found in Hebrews 13:20-21. For additional impact, write it down.

    b. What do you learn about God and Jesus?

3.   a. I find Hebrews 13:21 so encouraging, because I'm reminded of something very important. Read this verse. Who equips us and works in us for His glory?

    b. Compare this verse with Philippians 2:12-13. Why do we need to remember that He equips us and works in us?

    c. Think back to the believer's rest in Hebrews 4. What does it mean to be equipped for every good thing and at the same time be at rest in Jesus?

Reflect & Respond

These final verses are compelling as we take into consideration the 12 chapters that have gone before. We started with God speaking to us through His Son, and we end with the God of peace, the resurrected Shepherd. One last time the writer reminds us of the blood of the covenant as he exhorts us to do His will. What encourages me is that this great Shepherd of the sheep is the one who equips me to please Him.

@ Look at the following passages, and write down two or three things that please the Lord.
   II Corinthians 5:18-20

   Colossians 3:12-16

   I Thessalonians 4:1-7

@ Hebrews 13:21 tells us that He equips us to please Him. In other words, His Spirit, who lives in us, empowers us to do His will and to represent Him. Ephesians 5:18 says, "Don't get drunk with wine, for that is dissipation, but be filled with the Spirit." All of us, at the point of salvation, are indwelt by God's Spirit, and being filled with the Spirit means yielding to His control in every area of our lives. As you step into situations that challenge you, acknowledge the Lord, and ask Him to fill you with His Spirit. When you're in a conversation and you have no idea what to say, ask the Holy Spirit to fill you and give you His wisdom. When you're tempted to be impatient or unkind, call on the Spirit to fill you. The following verses encourage me to yield my heart and will to Jesus. Read them and write down what you discover about the Spirit's work in our lives:
   Acts 1:8

   Romans 8:26-27

   Galatians 3:3

DAY FIVE

Some Final Thoughts…

Congratulations, you're finished! Praise God for helping you complete your study of Hebrews. How I pray you've gained much more than you ever expected from your study of this great and complex book of the Bible. I pray you've grown deeper in your understanding of God's love and grace in your own life; and you've come to respect and worship Him with reverence and awe.

I remember writing at the beginning, "We'll never plumb the depths of this book of Scripture." As I wrap up this lesson, I'm acutely aware of the truth of that statement. Keep studying Hebrews over the course of your life. There's so much we didn't cover.

@ In Lesson One, I encouraged you to write down any questions you had about Hebrews. Look at your list to see if your questions have been answered. If not, let me encourage you to keep studying. I've used a number of commentaries throughout the study and recommend them for your use.

1 Graeme Goldsworthy Goldsworthy Trilogy (Sparksford, Patnernoster Press, 2000) p. 17.

2 Jonathon Edwards, *Personal Narrative*. (Online at www.graceonlinelibrary.com)

3 H.A. Ironside. *HEBREWS, JAMES, PETER.* (Philadelphia: American Bible Conference Association, 1932.) Page 172-173

BIBLIOGRAPHY

Baxter, J. Sidlow. *Going Deeper.*
    Chicago: Zondervan, 1959.

Buchanan, Mark. *The Rest of God*
    Nashville: W Publishing Group, 2006.

Buchanan, Mark. *Things Unseen.*
    Sisters: Multnomah Press, 2002.

Cook, Muriel. *Kitchen Table Counseling.*
    Colorado Springs: NavPress, 2006.

Dictionary.com used for definitions unless otherwise noted

Edwards, Jonathon. *Personal Narrative.*
    I need more info here too

Goldsworthy, Graeme. *Goldsworthy Trilogy.*
    Sparksford: Patnernoster Press, 2000.

Henry, Matthew. *Matthew Henry's Commentary on the Whole Bible*
    Hendrickson Online Publishers, 1991, 1994.

Ironside, H.A. *Hebrews-James-Peter.*
    Philadelphia: American Bible Conference Association, 1932.

Lewis, C.S. *The Last Battle*
    New York City: HarperCollins, 1994

Lloyd-Jones, Sally. *The Jesus Storybook Bible.*
    Grand Rapids: Zondervan, 2007.

MacArthur, John. *The MacArthur New Testament Commentary HEBREWS.*
    Chicago, Moody Press, 1983

Mahaney, C.J. *Living the Cross Centered Life.*
    Colorado Springs: Multnomah Books, 2006.

Piper, John. *The Passion of Jesus Christ.*
    Crossway, Wheaton. 2004.

Piper, John. *Seeing and Savoring Jesus Christ.*
    Wheaton: Crossway, 2004.

Piper, John. Sermon: *Jesus: Worthy of More Glory than Moses.*
    Need more info here 1996.

Ringma, Charles. *The Seeking Heart .*
    Brewster: Paraclete Press, 2006.

Stedman, *Ray Sermons on Hebrews*
    Online Commentary

Stowell, Joseph. *Following Christ.*
    Grand Rapids: Zonderva, 1996.

Wright, Tom. *Hebrews for Everyone.*
    London: Ashford Colour Press, 2003.

NOTES

NOTES

NOTES

NOTES

NOTES

AVAILABLE TITLES FROM CAS MONACO

Absolutely Free in Christ

A devotional Bible study on the book of Galatians

Absolutely Free in Christ provides an in-depth and thorough look at the book of Galatians and encourages believers to discover for themselves the source of true freedom in Christ.

Astonishing Love

A devotional Bible study on the book of First John with glimpses of the Gospel of John

This study of I John is designed to deepen your devotion to Jesus Christ and draw you closer to Him as you spend time in His Word. In addition to enhancing your personal walk with the Lord and exposing you to His astonishing love, you will learn the mark of authentic Christianity and the key ingredient to genuine Christian living.

Entrusting God's Treasure to the Faithful

Seven lessons on Biblical discipleship from II Timothy

This is discipleship made practical. Learn what it means to entrust God's treasure to the faithful by studying the book of II Timothy. This study also includes practical lessons on how to lead a Bible study, how to conduct an appointment with a disciple, and other valuable tools.

Living in the Riches of His Grace

A devotional Bible study on the book of Ephesians

Learn how to live in the riches of God's grace by studying the book of Ephesians. This study will help you unlock the secret to victorious Christian living.

Living Passionately for Christ

A devotional Bible study on the book of Philippians

This study is designed to ascertain the source of and the reason for passionate Christ-centered living. Discover what sets a believer apart and how such a believer will make an impact on the world—through relationships with family and friends, in the workplace, in sickness, and through affliction. Stretch the limits of your faith for the glory of God.

AVAILABLE TITLES FROM CAS MONACO

Standing Firm in a World of Opportunity

A devotional Bible study on the book of I Peter

First Peter guides us through trials, relationships, and opposition from the world. It reminds us that we are a chosen race, a royal priesthood, and a holy nation called to proclaim His excellencies in a world of opportunity.

*For ordering information, please visit www.entrusting.org or contact
Cas directly at (503) 750-8838 or Cas.Monaco@uscm.org*

Made in the USA
San Bernardino, CA
27 December 2013